T0343471

Physical Security Strategy and Process Playbook

John Kingsley-Hefty

ELSEVIER

AMSTERDAM · BOSTON · HEIDELBERG · LONDON
NEW YORK · OXFORD · PARIS · SAN DIEGO
SAN FRANCISCO · SINGAPORE · SYDNEY · TOKYO

Security
Executive Council

Elsevier
The Boulevard, Langford Lane, Kidlington, Oxford, OX5 1GB, UK
225 Wyman Street, Waltham, MA 02451, USA

First published 2013

Notices
Knowledge and best practice in this field are constantly changing. As new research and experience broaden our understanding, changes in research methods, professional practices, or medical treatment may become necessary.

Practitioners and researchers must always rely on their own experience and knowledge in evaluating and using any information, methods, compounds, or experiments described herein. In using such information or methods they should be mindful of their own safety and the safety of others, including parties for whom they have a professional responsibility.

To the fullest extent of the law, neither the Publisher nor the authors, contributors, or editors, assume any liability for any injury and/or damage to persons or property as a matter of products liability, negligence or otherwise, or from any use or operation of any methods, products, instructions, or ideas contained in the material herein.

British Library Cataloguing-in-Publication Data
A catalogue record for this book is available from the British Library

Library of Congress Cataloging-in-Publication Data
A catalog record for this book is available from the Library of Congress

ISBN: 978-0-12-417227-2

For more publications in the Elsevier Risk Management and Security Collection, visit our website at store.elsevier.com/SecurityExecutiveCouncil.

This book has been manufactured using Print On Demand technology. Each copy is produced to order and is limited to black ink. The online version of this book will show color figures where appropriate.

Working together
to grow libraries in
developing countries

www.elsevier.com • www.bookaid.org

CONTENTS

EXECUTIVE SUMMARY

Creating guidelines for effectively managing security risk involves a considerable amount of planning, effort, and cost. The *Physical Security Strategy and Process Playbook* provides the essentials you'll need to start filling in the pieces of prevention strategies that work for your organization.

In this playbook you will find instructions for identifying the particular security needs of your business and definitions of physical security concepts. It will also help you examine the operations, sites, and functional areas of your business and explore the most common security risks to each area. Lastly, this playbook includes guidelines for the implementation and evaluation of a physical security system and a description of the internal and external resources that are available to you.

WHAT IS A PLAYBOOK?

A playbook is an excellent tool for the security or business leader who wants to develop, implement, enhance, or validate a specific aspect of a security or risk management program. Playbooks provide a detailed treatment of a security program or service that can be quickly and effectively applied to an immediate need within an organization. Playbooks define and present the essential elements most often used by successful practitioners. They can also be used by non-security personnel who need an introduction and plan for action on a new security-related job responsibility. Playbooks are particularly useful for educators that are committed to providing current, relevant information and practices distilled from successful practitioners and programs and that have a direct correlation to current security positions.

INTRODUCTION

There is no one document that can be taken off the shelf and implemented in every business culture; however, it's possible to adapt the procedures and best practices discussed in this playbook, which has chapters categorized by issues, to create risk management guidelines that are customized to meet your unique needs. Although it includes some key elements that most companies have in common, this playbook does not cover sector-specific issues.

We recognize the existence of a wide variety of operations and security needs within your organization. Though the purpose of this playbook is to aid the security professional in addressing his or her physical security needs, those needs are undoubtedly unique, and this book cannot provide all the answers to every situation. This playbook can be used as an educational tool, it can help you define your security requirements, and it can serve as a reference for future planning.

As an educational tool, it can be used during planning for a specific security goal or in conjunction with a plan for a major change to your facility or business. You can use it to research solutions, to help you discuss your proposed solutions with management, and to develop a request for engineering assistance and budget.

You will also find this playbook useful as you develop the functional requirements of a security system that meets your goals and fits within your business operations. These functional requirements are essential for receiving assistance from management, engineering, and finance.

In addition, this playbook is a handy reference when you are planning for future changes, when you're talking to a security specialist, or if you need to find a resource.

The playbook is organized into six component parts around the central theme that physical security is part of sound business management.

1. An introduction to and explanation of basic physical security concepts.
2. A description of the probable security risks for each of the functional areas in your business.
3. Security performance guidelines along with a variety of supporting security options. The guidelines are flexible and the options can be modified to work within your particular business environment.
4. Performance specifications for the security options described in the chapter on security performance guidelines.
5. Security system selection, implementation, and evaluation guidelines that will help you reach the level of performance required.
6. Lists of the available resources that you can use as you plan and implement security measures.

The playbook is intended for people who are responsible for security-related decisions at your organization

- Security coordinators
- Security managers
- Facility, department, and unit Managers
- Managers responsible for choosing security solutions
- Information technology (IT) managers
- Engineering
- Information security coordinators
- Auditors
- Corporate real estate

The following chart shows you how to use this playbook to find information on a specific topic. You can read selected parts of some chapters and find help with a particular question without reading the entire text. The chart lists the chapter titles across the top of the page, with the steps you would follow in researching an issue flowing from the upper left corner to the lower right.

Chapter 1	Chapter 2	Chapter 3	Chapter 4	Chapter 5	Chapter 6
Physical Security Concepts	Functional Areas and Security Risks	Security Performance Guidelines and Options	Performance Specifications	Systems Implementation and Evaluation	Physical Security Resources
Understand the basic concepts ➔					
	Assess the risks to each area of your business ➔				
		Plan to minimize the risks ↓ Understand the Performance Guidelines ↓ Read the minimum security requirements and the recommended enhancements ↓ Identify appropriate security options ➔			
			Understand the performance specifications ➔		
				Prepare system plans and specifications ↓ Select a vendor ↓ Purchase equipment ↓ Install, turn on, and test the system ↓ Understand the system-related policies and procedures ➔	
					Use the available resources

There is one key policy and one essential set of procedures that provide the foundation for physical security. The key policy is your organization's access control and ID policy, which is discussed in Chapter 1. The set of essential procedures is embodied in the performance guidelines described in Chapter 3.

The *Physical Security Strategy and Process Playbook* should not be construed as a means to establish any legal standard of care or identify what reasonably prudent security precautions should be taken in any specific situation. The actions to be taken for individual situations will vary depending on the corporate culture and individual circumstances at the time. Ultimately, you must assess the situation, choose a response, and manage the consequences.

The material this playbook contains was devised over the course of twenty years, with updates as trends and risks changed. You may decide to combine it with other playbooks in the Elsevier Security Executive Council Risk Management Porfolio such as the *Workplace Security Playbook, Personal Safety and Security Playbook*, and *Business Continuity Playbook* to build a complete, A-to-Z security manual.

Physical Security Concepts

1.1 BEFORE YOU BEGIN

Before you implement any physical security measures, you should understand the fundamental concepts in three areas. These areas are:

1. Assessing the security risks to your business.
2. Zones of protection.
3. Components of a security system: barriers, technology, procedures, and people.

As you work through the concepts in each of these areas, you will be able to answer the basic physical security questions: What is the goal of my current system? Is my system accomplishing its objectives? Why or why not? What, if anything, do I need to change? Are there other ways I can meet my goals?

1.1.1 What are your Security Goals?

Before you begin assessment of your security system, you need to know your security goals. All of your security activities should support these goals. If you don't have a clear understanding of your goals, you will not be able to implement a cost effective system that meets your needs.

A clear statement of your security goals is usually built on answers to questions like the following:

- Do I want to correct a problem or reduce a potential risk?
- Do my proposed solutions address the needs that I have identified?
- Are my solutions consistent with the business culture?
- Will the solutions hinder business operations?
- Will the solutions enhance security performance guidelines for the business?
- Is new technology part of the solution?
- Is the new technology consistent with the long range plans of the business?

1.2 ASSESSING THE NEEDS OF YOUR BUSINESS

Physical security must make sense within the context of your business operations. In order to build a security system that works for any business, the needs of that business must first be assessed.

At the core of this assessment are the following operational issues:

- What is the general level of risk for this business?
- What are the critical events that will stop this business?
- What are the products, information, and assets at this site? What specific risks are associated with each of them?
- How do people and materials enter and leave?
- What are the work schedules?

We often recommend a **security assessment** as the first step in assessing the needs of your business. This helps you arrive at an overall assessment of the security issues relating to your business operations—your people, information, property, product, and the corporation's reputation.

In order to use a security assessment properly, you first need to understand the three fundamental elements of security: probability, criticality, and vulnerability. The next section describes how an effective security assessment is based on these three concepts.

1.2.1 Elements of Security

An effective security assessment applies an understanding of the fundamental elements of security to a particular location or area within the business. As you look at each area, you must consider the following questions:

- What is the probability of a security-related incident occurring in this area?
- How critical might the incident be to my business operations?
- How vulnerable is the area to a security incident?

Answers to these questions help you to arrive at an assessment of the level of security risk associated with a particular area of your business.

1.2.1.1 Element 1: Probability

Probability is the likelihood that a security incident will occur, independent of any effort you may make to avoid the incident. Probability is affected by factors such as your location and environment, your product, the personnel at your site, and other factors that are essentially beyond your control.

For example, if your facility is located in a high-density area of a large city, the probability of parking lot incidents and vandalism is much greater than if your facility is located in a small rural town. Or, if you use a proprietary process or have proprietary information that has a high market value, you are more likely to have theft attempts than if you don't use such a process or possess such information.

As you perform a security assessment, keep in mind that each area of your business must be evaluated in terms of the probability that security incidents will occur there. As you assess each area of your business, make a list of the most frequent incidents that have occurred in your building, at your location, and in the surrounding area or neighborhood.

1.2.1.2 Element 2: Criticality
The criticality of a security incident is the degree to which it affects your ability to do business. An incident with high criticality is one that:

- Interrupts your business operations;
- Has significant operational or legal ramifications;
- Impacts or reduces sales;
- Erodes the quality of your products or services;
- Gives the competition a significant advantage;
- Causes the loss of substantial revenue; and/or
- Damages the corporation's reputation.

As you assess each area of your business, make a list of the security incidents that could have a high degree of criticality.

1.2.1.3 Element 3: Vulnerability
Vulnerability is a measure of your ability to prevent a security incident. Your current security system and procedures represent the active steps you've taken to decrease your vulnerability.

Vulnerability is a dynamic concept. It changes whenever your environment, operations, personnel, business and/or systems change. Each time a substantive security-related change occurs in an area of your business, you need to reconsider your vulnerability in that area.

As you assess your business, keep track of the things that make it easier to reduce the likelihood that an incident will occur, as well as the ones that make it more difficult.

1.2.2 Combining the Three Elements of Security to Arrive at an Assessment of Risk

The most cost-effective security systems consider all three elements of security simultaneously to arrive at an assessment of the risk associated with a particular area. As shown in Figure 1.1, you can gauge the overall security risk for an area by determining the degree to which the area has high values for probability, criticality, and vulnerability.

It makes most sense to concentrate your resources on areas that have the greatest degree of security risk. Highest priority should be given to those areas that have high values for probability, criticality, and vulnerability.

When the values for a particular area add up to an unacceptable level of risk, it is vital that you lower one or more of them by implementing security measures. On the other hand, areas

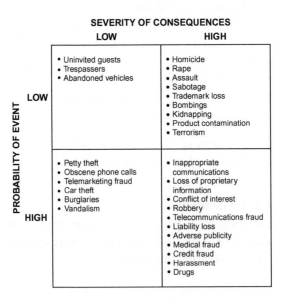

Figure 1.1 Security Risk Matrix.

that have a uniform set of low values should not be using security resources that could be better spent in other areas of your business.

1.2.3 Matrix of Security Risks

Another way to look at security risks is to create a matrix of four quadrants. The quadrants are based on two high–low dimensions: 1) the probability that a particular event will occur, and, 2) the severity of the consequences should the event actually take place.

Figure 1.1 classifies many of the events that could happen at your business by placing them in the appropriate quadrant. You may want to classify these and other events for your business by completing an exercise similar to the example below.

1.2.4 Deterrence: Creating an Effective Security Zone

The best security methods prevent incidents before they happen. For the most part, incidents can be avoided by creating a security zone in which individuals considering a security violation realize that the probability of being detected and identified is far greater than the reward they can expect to gain from the violation.

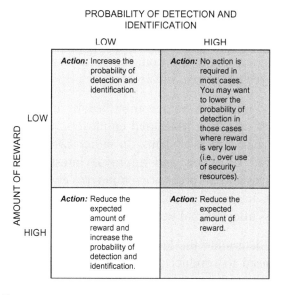

Figure 1.2 Security Zones.

Figure 1.2 shows how two factors—probability of detection and identification and expected amount of reward—interact to produce areas of effective and ineffective security zones.

The most effective security zones (shown in darker gray) have a high probability of detection and identification and a low amount of expected reward. Moderately effective zones (shown in lighter gray) and ineffective security zones (shown in white) can be enhanced by increasing the probability of detection and identification, lowering the amount of expected reward, or doing both.

1.2.5 Your Organization's Corporate Access Control and ID Policy

Access control is the cornerstone of any operation's security program. It is the most critical element for preventing incidents and responding to emergencies.

Access control must be designed to accommodate different levels of risk. Most of the systems and procedures are designed to handle the daily routine needs of controlling access. However, the ability to escalate the level of control must be built into the system so that high-risk threats can also be handled effectively.

It is security's responsibility to control physical access to all your organization's facilities. This includes properties, buildings, offices, and business-critical system infrastructures. Access control applies to: employees assigned to the location, temporary employees, customers, contract employees, vendors, and visitors.

Acceptable control can be accomplished by utilizing receptionists, security officers, or other designated employees, alone or in conjunction with electronic access systems. In either case, a manual or electronic audit trail of access and approvals must be maintained for visiting employees and all other non-employees entering your organization's property. In addition, an audit trail must be maintained for all employee access after normal business hours.

In order to determine the level of access control required by your business, you need to conduct a security assessment. In the following section, procedures for conducting a security assessment are discussed.

1.2.6 Security Assessment

A security assessment consists of questions focused on eight main areas of your business. The answers to these questions will help you determine the security measures that are most cost effective and sensible for your business.

The eight areas of a security assessment include:

1. Location and local environment
2. Facility profile
3. Operations and products
4. Business functions
5. Potential security concerns
6. Security history
7. Current level of protection
8. Plan for upgrades

Each of these areas is discussed in detail in the sections that follow. As you read through the sections and answer the questions, consider the relative impact of each of your answers on your overall security risk.

1.2.6.1 Location and Local Environment

The geographic and social environment surrounding your facility is a major security concern.

- What types of natural disasters have occurred or can be expected in your area? What is the probability of each of these occurring?
- What's the overall crime rate of the surrounding community?
- How far away is the nearest major city?
- What is quality of the response by police and fire departments? How quickly do they respond?
- How close is the nearest residential neighborhood?
- Do your business neighbors have a high level of security risk (for example, military contractors, animal research operations, hazardous materials or processes, high-value businesses such as electronics or negotiables, companies targeted by social or environmental activists)?
- Is your facility as secure as your business neighbors'? Or, does it look like the easiest target in the area?
- Is there a college or university within the community?

As you classify the environment around your business, be aware that the environment can change quickly, especially during a period of civil unrest.

1.2.6.2 Facility
This area focuses on the buildings and work space in which your business operates.

- How many buildings make up your facility? What are the dimensions of these buildings? Are they all in the same location?
- How long do you plan to stay in your present location?
- Are you planning any renovations or expansions?
- Is the facility owned or leased?
- Does the facility have tenants other than your business?
- What is the replacement value of the facility?
- How many entrances must be functional in order for your business to operate?
- What is the volume of non-employee traffic at each of the entrances?
- What control systems (security equipment and procedures) are currently in place in the facility?
- Where do employees and visitors park? How safe is it?

1.2.6.3 Operations and Products
To understand the security issues relating to your operations and products, gather the following information.

Operations

- Number of employees
- Average length of service
- Number of female employees (and percent of the total)
- Employee absentee rate
- Employee turnover rate
- Number of union and non-union employees, exempt and non-exempt
- If union, number and type of grievances registered over the last three years
- Number of shifts per week
- Number and type of suspensions over the last three years
- Number of and reason for terminations over the last three years
- Assessment of employee morale

- Visitor/vendor/contractor volume (number of people per day)
- Shipping and receiving truck volume (number of vehicles per day)
- Amount of access required during non-business hours

Products

- Value and market appeal of your products
- Production volumes and inventory levels
- Product portability
- Secondary product uses
- Resale value
- Distribution channels

1.2.6.4 Business Functions

Each type of business function and corporate asset has its own security-related concerns. Corporate assets are defined as people, products, property, information, and company reputation. Which of the following functions are performed at your operation, and which assets that require protection are at risk and require additional protection?

- Manufacturing
- Sales
- Marketing
- Administration
- Distribution and warehousing
- Computer operations
- Research and development

A facilities profile form should be used to help document the security concerns relating to your business functions. Keep a permanent record of this information and update it each year; any pertinent information that is not recorded on the facilities profile form should be recorded elsewhere and updated annually.

1.2.6.5 Potential Security Concerns

The following list identifies business issues with potential security risks. It should be noted that these issues are dynamic; they must be continually reviewed as local conditions and operations change.

- Business changes that cause people in the workplace to experience significant change. For example:
  - Acquisition/integration

- Down-sizing or divestiture
- Disciplinary actions and terminations
- Completion of projects
- Increase in publicity about your organization's operations
- Operations or product production capabilities that are one-of-a-kind
- Limited recovery/backup capability
- Computer room(s) on the premises
- Security system(s) environment, equipment, and network(s) on site
- Computer system(s) not integrated with your organization's corporate systems
- Contingency plans in place for information loss
- Hazardous materials or hazardous wastes on site
- Potential for employee sabotage
- Product contamination potential
- Products have high street value and appeal
- Proprietary information located at your site — how critical to your business is this information?

1.2.6.6 Security History
Looking over your security history helps you to be more aware of future security risks. Gather the historical information described in the list below, along with any other security-related history that may help you identify trends and assess probabilities.

- Number and type of reported security incidents on or near your organization's property over last three years
- Number and type of parking lot incidents
- History or suspicion of drug problems (use or sale)
- History of employee, vendor, contractor, and visitor theft
- Number of sabotage incidents over the last three years
- Number of bomb threats or inappropriate communications over the last three years
- Number of domestic or workplace violence incidents
- Community crime problems
- Number of unauthorized people discovered on your site
- The degree to which you suspect you've lost information from your site
- The number of incidents where coordination of local emergency service (police, fire, ambulance) was required

1.2.6.7 Current Level of Protection

Only after you've completed the risk assessment process will you be able to evaluate the adequacy of your current level of protection. The following list of security items may or may not be present at your site, so some may not be appropriate, while some may be appropriate but are not fully implemented.

- Can and do you control access to your operations in accordance with your organization's access control and ID policy?
- Can your level of access control be strengthened to accommodate emergency situations or times of increased risk due to competitors' intelligence gathering, attempts by social activists to gain entry, or attempts by disgruntled former workers to gain access?
- How many interior and exterior cameras are deployed on your current video system? Are the cameras analog or IP digital? Are they adequate for your current operations?
- Do you have an approved employee ID program? If yes, are these IDs electronic and a component of the access control system, or do you use a separate electronic element for electronic access control entry?
- Is your visitor/contractor badge system used uniformly?
- Do the perimeter entry points meet the needs of the current operations?
- Are your fences and gates controlled?
- Do you have an interior alarm system? If yes, do your current interior sensing technologies and system accommodate flexible work-schedule environments, or should you upgrade your system?
- What is your key control system? Is its integrity intact?
- Have you deployed a removable core locking cylinder system for rapid security adjustments?
- Have you deployed an electronic access control key-dispensing system for critical areas under control?
- Do you use CCTV? Is your video IP-based on your organization's network and switch? Does it record events? Is it monitored?
- Do you have security officers? Do they have adequate written policies and procedures? Are they trained?
- Is there an emergency management plan for your facility?
- Do you have adequate exterior and interior signage and postings? Is it written and posted in accordance with your organization's inspection guidelines?
- How many security awareness programs do you have each year?

- Do you maintain a working relationship with emergency security services in your community? Do they respond quickly to your requests? Do local police provide adequate patrols?

1.2.6.8 Plan for Upgrades

As your needs change and as technology changes, plan for upgrades to your security systems. It may not be sufficient to simply replace old equipment; an equipment upgrade may be required.

- Determine the effective lifespan of your equipment.
- Review new technologies when the time arrives to upgrade or replace your equipment.
- Use preventative maintenance to extend the effective life of equipment and materials.

1.2.7 Ongoing Security Assessments

Over time, things change. You may notice an increase in minor security incidents at your facility, or you may not notice anything until there is an emergency. However, if you routinely perform a security assessment of your facility, you will be more prepared to handle any type of security incident.

1.2.8 Introduction to Performance Guidelines

The assessment process outlined in the previous sections will help supplement your existing security program where necessary, as well as provide a framework for planning for the future of your business operations and security needs.

An effective security plan is essential for operating within your organization's security performance guidelines. Before you can build such a plan, you need to be familiar with the performance guidelines that drive the plan.

1.2.9 Performance Guidelines

Performance guidelines specify the required outcomes from a set of security measures. The guidelines will be based on the reality of your organization's various business operations, since the diversity of your businesses and sites may make it impractical to list uniform standards that will work for all locations. Instead, we have defined levels of performance that your security programs should meet for specific areas of your business.

Every area of a facility should have performance guidelines: the parking lot, reception area, cafeteria, computer room, laboratory, and electrical closet, to name a few. The performance requirement for an area defines the minimum security needs for that area.

Once you know the performance guidelines for an area, you can select the security measures that will both fulfill the requirement and meet the specific objectives of your facility.

Security is every employee's responsibility. However, your employees can best implement and maintain the security measures at your facility when you have taken the steps necessary to integrate security into your business operations.

1.2.10 Your Organization's Overall Security Performance Guidelines

As you assess your business needs, remember that your overall security goal is to provide appropriate levels of security for protecting people, property, information, assets, and your organization's reputation.

To provide the appropriate levels of protection for your operations, follow these eight performance guidelines.

1. **Identify your security needs**. Identify the areas and levels of security you need.
2. **Integrate security**. Integrate security into your environment and business operations.
3. **Control physical access**. Control physical access to your site, buildings, and offices.
4. **Control information access**. Control access to your proprietary information.
5. **Detect unauthorized access**. Detect unauthorized access to your site or your information.
6. **Be prepared for an incident**. Prepare for incidents and emergencies.
7. **Respond effectively**. Respond quickly and effectively to incidents and emergencies.
8. **Report promptly**. Report incidents promptly and correctly.

1.3 ZONES OF PROTECTION

For purposes of security, your operations, both on a macro and a micro level, can be divided into four zones. The zones generally are thought of as concentric circles—each zone refers to the contents of the physical area within the circle.

A zone forms a line of protection; it is used to identify the security level required for a particular area:

- Zone One refers to the property on which the building is located.
- Zone Two refers to the building perimeter and its facade. This includes all the entry points to the inside of the building, such as doors and windows.
- Zone Three refers to the "open" interior areas within the building such as reception areas, lobbies, halls, cafeterias, and open office spaces. This zone can also refer to those areas located in Zone One that require greater access control and tighter security measures (for example, equipment areas, storage facilities, or parking areas).
- Zone Four refers to those high-security areas where only very limited access is allowed. These areas are usually within the building, such as a computer room or laboratory, but they can also be located outside the building. Power generating equipment, communications equipment, chemical tanks, and hazardous material storage all might qualify as Zone Four areas.

The application of multiple zones, in a series of concentric circles, provides for increasing security as you move toward the center. Each subsequent zone adds another level of protection to your operation's overall security system.

Figure 1.3 shows how the zones are usually visualized. Although the zones move inward from the perimeter, it is often possible to have zones of higher value located in areas of lower value. For example, information stored on a portable computer or on a home computer needs Zone Four protection, even though it is clearly outside of Zone One.

For many offices and laboratories, the reception area to the building is an extension of the boundary for Zone One. The common areas, hallways, and conference rooms are in Zone Two. Each person's office or cubicle is in Zone Three. Cabinets, desks, computers, and special rooms are in Zone Four.

As with all forms of security, it is the responsibility of all personnel (employees, supervisors, managers) to follow the security procedures appropriate to each zone of protection.

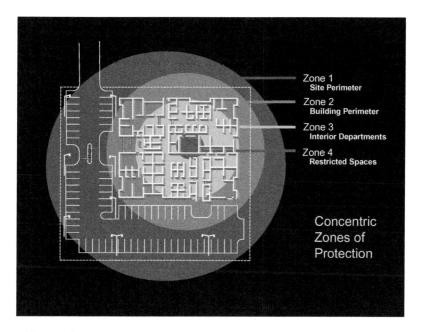

Figure 1.3 Layers of Security.

1.4 SECURITY COMPONENTS

Security systems are made up of four main components, each of which must be integrated with the others:

1. Physical barriers
2. Technology
3. People
4. Policies and procedures

The components can be very different, depending on the location of your business. The physical barriers and the technology used in your system depend on your needs. The people and policies and procedures you employ are very specific to the culture of your business environment.

Your security system must constantly be tuned so that it is a coherent part of your local environment and your operation's assessed risk. For example, laboratories have different needs than sales, medical materials production is very different from production of industrial minerals. Regional architectural differences between northern and southern climates play a large role in planning a security system. The cultural differences between the United States, Colombia, Indonesia,

Europe, and South Africa also have a profound impact on the design of a cost-effective security system for each location.

The effectiveness of a security system depends on how well its components are integrated into its overall design. Integrating components into the whole is called layering; it refers to the method of overlapping components and creating redundancy so that the system has no weak points. We will discuss the details of system integration and layering in a later section.

1.4.1 Physical Barriers

Physical barriers are used to form perimeter lines of defense. They can successfully deter an intruder, though you should count on them only to delay the intruder. Fences, for example, can usually be compromised within one minute.

At your facilities, use physical barriers in each of their zones of protection. Some examples of the barriers used in each zone include the following:

- Exterior (Zone One): Natural terrain, landscaping, fencing, gates, walls, and notification and warning signs.
- Building Perimeter (Zone Two): Building walls, doors, gates, windows, roofs, hatches, access panels, grills, grates, and notification and warning signs.
- Building Interior (Zone Three): Partition walls, furniture partitions, doors, gates, glass panels, railings, floors, ceilings, access panels, grills, notification and warning signs.
- Restricted Areas (Zone Four): Any of the physical barriers used in the other zones, plus some form of fencing, walls, and restrictive access; notification and warning signs; locking cabinets for proprietary materials and information; and vaults with combination locks.

1.4.2 Technology and Control Systems

Technology and control systems are used in a physical security system to monitor and secure the environment and to detect intrusion. The control systems options for your organization's facilities include the following:

- Exterior (Zone One): Locks and keys, perimeter alarms, motion detection, CCTV, instructional signs, security officers, electronic access controls, and lighting.

- Building Perimeter (Zone Two): Locks and keys, alarms, annunciation, motion detection, warning lights, electronic access controls, CCTV, security officers, receptionists, other assigned people, instructional signs, employee badge/ID systems, and visitor badge systems.
- Building Interior (Zone Three): Lock and keys, alarms, annunciation, motion detection, electronic access controls, CCTV, security officers, receptionists, other assigned people, instructional signs, employee badge/ID systems, and visitor badge systems.
- Restricted Areas (Zone Four): Same as Zone Three, with the additional precaution of a dedicated control system, including a dedicated response, provided for the restricted area. Additional Zone Four precautions include alarm monitoring devices, escorted access to restricted areas, full audit trail of all access, password or PIN number protections, and biometric verification.

1.4.3 The Human Component

Systems do not stand alone. People are responsible for ensuring that technology is applied appropriately, systems are monitored and maintained, and responses are made to events that call for action. A card access system is not effective, for example, if authorized personnel hold doors open for unauthorized personnel, and management does not monitor and correct the system.

Installing a security system does not guarantee that your security goals will be met. A system that is installed for appearances only creates both a false sense of security and a host of legal issues.

1.4.4 People: The Trusted Person System

People are the cornerstone and collective strength of the security system at every organizational facility, building, and operation. Effective security depends more on the awareness and support of the people in the workplace than on technology.

People are trusted to perform their jobs with integrity. We know that the vast majority of people in the workplace have a high degree of loyalty and dedication. It is critical that people are made aware of the risks to security associated with their work and understand their responsibilities for maintaining a safe and secure workplace.

- Policies and procedures: The actual implementation of a physical security program consists of policies and procedures. The degree to which people follow and support these policies and procedures determines the success of the operation's security system.
- Systems management: People are responsible for insuring that all components of a security system work together to provide comprehensive and consistent coverage and that the system is performing to its full capacity and delivering its desired results.
- Now that security systems have evolved into digital networked platforms, all of your organization's computer devices should follow applied standards. Partnerships between security and IT are now the norm. Maintaining security systems requires a "steady state" condition to ensure the systems' 24−7 reliability. If the security system(s) are on the your organization's network, a partnership with your organization's IT is essential.
- Training: Training and education programs keep people informed about potential security risks, teach them physical security procedures and techniques, show them how to respond in case an incident occurs, and ensures that everyone knows what resources are available. Systems training keeps people aware of ways to detect potential problems and ways to correct them. Training must also focus on equipment operation and maintenance, as well as providing cross-training so that relief personnel are available.
- Monitoring: All security systems (ID badges, cameras, alarms, access control systems, and so on) must be monitored consistently to be effective. In addition, a program of designed responses to information gathered by the monitoring process is essential to the system's success.
- Response to alarms: A quick, consistent response to every alarm situation shows that the operation is serious about enforcing security procedures and protecting your organization's assets.
- Informational reports and activity reports: These reports must be reviewed to identify any problems there might be with the security system. Follow-up and corrective actions must be taken when problems are identified.
- Validation testing: All systems must be periodically tested to ensure functionality and, more importantly, performance. Validation testing consists of getting answers to questions such as: Do the right people take the correct action when an alarm situation occurs? Are

visitors being stopped and signed in? Are ID badges being worn and checked? Do alarms sound when doors are opened?

1.4.5 Responsibility for Critical System Components

Security is the shared responsibility of everyone within an organization. Some people, however, will be more actively engaged in security-related activities. They have security-related responsibilities as a part of their job descriptions. Other employees have a more secondary role. These people practice personal awareness and take an active role in the protection of your organization's assets.

Critical components of a security system must be assigned as specific responsibilities to individuals. The effectiveness of these individuals' performance must be evaluated on a regular basis, as part of their PADP (performance appraisal and development program). The critical areas that should be assigned to an individual as part of their professional responsibility are:

- Systems management
- Systems maintenance
- Systems training
- Monitoring
- Response
- Information and activity reports
- Policies and procedures
- Personal security awareness
- Validation testing

Each of these system components crosses over the zones of protection described earlier in this chapter. The people responsible for these critical aspects of the security system cannot confine their concerns to a single zone—the strength of the system depends on its components being well integrated.

1.4.6 Employee Responsibilities

Keep the human component in mind as you evaluate your current system and plan for any changes. People are a critical part of any security system that both provides effective business protection and meets operational needs.

The following tables list, for each type of security component or technology, the responsibilities that must be assigned to individual employees. As you consider each of the following security components and technologies, keep in mind that you should coordinate your assessment and planning activities with your organization's security representative.

Alarm Systems

- Create a local and a central monitoring station.
- Establish and document policies and procedures for all aspects of the system.
- Establish and maintain the authorized access list and times of access.
- Inform employees of the existence of the system (if it is new) and tell them what to do when an alarm sounds.
- Provide system training as needed.
- Respond to all alarms.
- Validate that the system is operating as designed and people are responding according to established procedures.
- Generate activity and exception reports. Analyze them for patterns.
- Follow up on problems and exceptions that are reported.
- Test and inspect the system.
- Provide for system maintenance. Fine tune the system.

Badging Systems and Visitor Escort

- Communicate and implement an access control and ID policy.
- Establish and document policies and procedures.
- Define operation's access hours.
- Differentiate between employees, contractors, and visitors by defining the access rights of each group.
- Train employees to recognize and respond to people who are not following the established procedures.
- Provide escorts.
- Design validation tests and use them to ensure systems integrity.
- Determine the appropriate responses for recovery of badges and visitor credentials.
- Manage and recover lost, stolen, or duplicate credentials.

Card Access Systems

- Provide system training as needed.
- Establish and document policies and procedures for all aspects of the system.
- Enter data and maintain the records.
- Keep the system current by accounting for all the cards issued.
- Generate activity reports and analyze them.
- Follow up on problems and exceptions that are reported.
- Provide for system maintenance and IT "steady state" support.
- Validate that the system is operating as designed and people are responding according to established procedures.

Closed-Circuit Television (CCTV)

- Establish and document policies and procedures for monitoring, response, and maintenance, and assign responsibility.
- Inform employees of the existence of the system (if it is new) and tell them its purposes and limitations.
- Provide system training as needed.
- Monitor and record activity.
- Test and inspect the system.
- Generate activity and exception reports. Analyze them for patterns.
- Follow up on problems and exceptions that are reported.
- Validate that the system is operating as designed and people are responding according to established procedures.

Lighting

- Establish and document policies and procedures and assign responsibility.
- Measure lighting levels for compliance with national engineering standards.
- Bring all lighting levels into compliance.
- Inspect and maintain lights on a regular basis.

Locking Devices and Key Control

- Establish and document policies and procedures on use, applications, and key control.
- Decide whether to use keys or combination locks.
- Create and maintain lists of people authorized for each key or combination.
- Assess system integrity through validation tests.
- Recover keys; rekey locks and consider the use of removable cores to periodically rekey the mechanical locking system and change combinations as necessary.

Security Coordination, Systems Integration, and Employee Awareness

- Establish and document policies and procedures for control and responsibility of security systems.
- Determine staffing requirements, provide for training and cross-training, and for backup.
- Provide employee awareness programs.
- Test system integration.

1.5 INTEGRATING SYSTEMS

Achieving an integrated system is the goal of all physical security efforts. An integrated system incorporates planning, technology, people, and procedures in a way that provides optimum performance in a cost-effective way. An integrated system relies both on good design and careful maintenance.

The elements most commonly omitted from the integration process include the following:

- Master planning
- Layering
- Design review
- Operational systems review
- Reviews by the Security Committee
- Coordination with your organization's security representative

1.5.1 Master Planning

Master planning means taking a long-term, big-picture approach to defining problems and their solutions. The expertise of a security professional on your planning team or an outside security consultant can prove useful in assessing your current security needs and forecasting future requirements.

Experience has shown that when a particular facility chooses to go it alone when they define their security requirements, they often develop security systems that are over-designed, under-designed, misapplied, or that overlook some security needs entirely. As a result, retro-fitting and reengineering such a system at a later date can be an expensive proposition.

Using a master plan gives you a framework for evaluating security requirements and solutions. It is essential that you identify all your facility's assets and the threats to them—not just the basic security deficiencies and remedies—before a systems solution can be engineered. You need to be careful that you don't prematurely expend resources that may address only the highly visible assets and threats to them.

1.5.2 Layering

Physical security systems must be designed in depth. Physical barriers, technology, people, and procedures must be creatively overlapped so that the protection system is layered.

Layering provides both diversity and redundancy. Diversity provides cross-checks on a situation while redundancy insures that every component is backed up in case of failure. Layering must be designed into the system. If layering is not part of the design, it's nearly impossible for the components to perform optimally in relation to the system's objectives.

Some examples of layering include the following:

- Magnetic door contacts, which are tested on a regular schedule, are used to monitor door alarms. Should there be a failure or undetected tampering, security personnel performing routine integrity testing of the door and its alarms will detect the failure.
- A card access system is installed to restrict access to authorized card holders. Any unauthorized use of the card is recorded by CCTV, which provides a video audit trail of the activity.

1.5.3 Design Review Prior to Investment Proposal

Before you request funds to spend on a new or upgraded security system, go through a design review with your organization's security representative to ensure that:

- The proper definition, including design study documents, have been compiled to address the security requirements for the project at hand, as well as integrating the project into the business' security master plan;
- The system is designed to meet all the security and operational needs;
- Adequate forecasting of funds is included in the investment proposal; and
- The appropriate equipment, product specifications, and configurations have been selected to meet the defined functional requirements of the project.

1.5.4 Operational Systems Review

Periodically, bring in your security specialist to review your operational security and your facility's security classification. Be certain to include:

- Your security committee's input;
- Any planned operational and security changes within the facility; and
- Any planned reassessment of the facility's integrated security system.

The goal of these operational reviews is to assess your system's effectiveness in meeting your business' present and near future security and operational needs.

1.5.5 Facility Security Committee and Reviews

Be certain to include your security committee in all reviews. The committee should meet at least once per quarter to establish a proactive approach to your security needs.

- Reviews provide an opportunity to anticipate and evaluate the impact of proposed physical and/or operational changes. You want to ensure that changes will not adversely compromise your overall security objectives and/or physical security systems.

- Reviews are a forum wherein the performance of your present security system can be evaluated and future security expectations can be defined.
- Reviews help to identify the personnel issues and the human element problems associated with maintaining an integrated system.

1.5.6 Working with Your Organization's Security Services

If you belong to a large corporation, it's likely that a corporate security team exists and can serve as a resource for your location-specific security needs. Corporate security, working together with your organization's staff groups, will help you identify the measures that help you achieve your security goals. They can also assist in your selection of a security coordinator.

CHAPTER 2

Functional Areas and Security Risks

2.1 INTRODUCTION

This chapter reviews the operations, sites, and functional areas of your business and explores the most common security risks to each area. Every facet of your business has potential security risks—the risks span the spectrum from theft to legal liability to loss of the company's reputation and way of life.

The risks discussed in this chapter are based on your organization's experience, the experience of related industries, and corporate priorities. Each of these risks can be addressed through the application of your organization's security performance guidelines and options, which will be discussed in Chapter 3.

This chapter is organized alphabetically by functional area, with the potential security risks for each area given. Use the lists to help you review your business operations. If you find risks that are applicable to your situation, and if you choose to take action to reduce or remove a risk, refer to Chapter 3 for assistance with the planning process for the specific areas that need improvement.

2.2 ASSESSMENT REVIEW

As you assess the risks to each area of your business, you should start by looking at the items that, in one way or another, concern all the areas of your business. A security assessment is essential when new construction or major remodeling is being planned.

It is also very useful to complete an assessment for an existing business in a facility that is not undergoing construction changes. The assessment will help identify security risks you may have overlooked and help you select options for meeting the performance guidelines.

Every attempt should be made to understand and plan for the security-related issues described in the next five sections:

1. Site analysis
2. Allocation of space
3. Compartmentalization
4. Adjacency factors
5. Circulation between buildings and areas

Once you understand the concepts contained in these sections, you'll have a solid foundation for making decisions about security at a detailed level.

2.2.1 Site Analysis (Office or Facility)

A site analysis is a joint effort between division management, facility management, and security. The process can be applied to a small office environment, a department, or an entire facility.

The goal of a site analysis is to collect pertinent information about the site's environment because the environment has such a large effect on the type and cost of the site's physical security systems. A site analysis can also be used to help select an environment that is suitable to the needs of your business operations.

The following topics are covered in a site analysis:

- Social and political factors: the degree to which the public is sensitive to the business's product, operation, or process.
- Criminal activities in the area: a crime analysis that provides uniform crime statistics.
- Neighboring properties, demographics, and environmental impact: includes neighbors, demographics of the surrounding area, risk of natural disasters, and the impact your business will have on the environment.
- Loss history: a summary of the history of loss suffered by the company currently operating at the site.
- Physical factors: including location, proximity to freeways and to major urban areas, the size of the land parcel, site access, and vehicular and pedestrian circulation.

2.2.2 Allocation of Space

Each operational unit within the facility has specific security requirements, which must be considered during the initial planning stage.

- Areas that interact with the public, such as purchasing, employment, and sales, should not be located inside highly secured areas of the facility. This creates unnecessary and non-secure circulation patterns for visitors and employees.
- Whenever possible, concentrate on areas that interact with the public within one building, wing, or floor. Provide a separate entrance, restrooms, and conference rooms for these areas. You'll be able to reduce the cost and inconvenience of the additional security controls required when public areas are intermingled with employee areas.

2.2.3 Compartmentalization

Although there is a trend toward more open work environments, be aware that there may be security risks associated with environments that are too open. These environments may still require compartmentalization.

- Often it is not practical, from a security standpoint, to locate research and development labs close to sales and marketing if the volume of non-employee traffic is high. Even though it may help these groups of employees communicate with each other, it may be very difficult to maintain a proper level of security.
- Consider the effects of having employee areas close to non-employee areas. You may find it difficult to protect sensitive information when non-employee areas are too close to employee areas. For example, if you bring customers to your site to provide training, create a training area that is separate from other areas that are difficult to protect.
- Be aware that an open work environment has additional security risks that surface during non-business hours. For example, it is difficult to guard against unauthorized use of equipment, records, and/or information if access is not restricted during non-business hours.

2.2.4 Adjacency Factors

Adjacency factors are related to the overall structure of the work environment. It makes good security sense to keep some areas close to each other, or close to the public. On the other hand, some other areas need to be separated from each other, or removed from the public.

- Human resources and purchasing functions should generally be near the visitor entrance because these areas tend to have high volumes of non-employee traffic.
- Computer rooms should be isolated, since relatively few people need to be in these rooms.
- Shipping and receiving areas should be separated from each other and from most employee and visitor traffic. In addition, they should have good access to roadways.
- Meeting rooms and auditoriums for special or public events should be located in areas designed for public access control.

2.2.5 Circulation Between Buildings and Areas

Besides allocating space for the various business functions, you need to plan out how people will move within and between buildings and areas. Inadvertent security risks are often caused by traffic patterns that are not based on a business need to be in the area. For example, people sometimes walk through a department that is unrelated to their business need because the only path (or shortest path) leading to their destination takes them through the unrelated department.

- Circulation patterns should separate the highly secured areas from nonsecured areas (i.e., restricted employee areas from visitor areas). The highly secured areas should also be separate from the traffic paths used most frequently by employees.
- Plan out the circulation patterns between buildings so that people can move safely and efficiently from place to place without compromising security. Efficient circulation reduces the probability of exposing your business and your people to unnecessary risk.
- Place departments that interact regularly next to each other, if possible, to reduce unnecessary traffic from employees and visitors.
- Provide direct access to parking areas. Be certain that paths to parking areas do not pass through hazardous areas.

2.3 RISKS BY AREA

This section is designed as a guide to help you identify the risks you might find in the different areas of your business. The areas listed in this section are functions, physical locations, and processes common to many organizations' business operations.

Based on our experience, we address the risks we have often found to be associated with each area, although the discussion is not all-inclusive. The degree of risk you find in each area of your business is highly dependent on the nature of your operations and on your location.

2.3.1 Access to Property

Review your access controls to determine all possible means of access for invited guests, uninvited guests, employees, contractors, vendors, and visitors.

The main considerations relating to access to your property are

- Theft, vandalism, sabotage, and assault;
- Accidental injury;
- Lack of preventative maintenance of control or safety devices;
- Unauthorized use or access;
- Animals on the premises;
- Lack of warning and directional signs;
- Barriers that are not effective;
- Access to hazardous materials; and
- Traffic flow that is not conducive to effective security.

2.3.2 Building Perimeter

In the past, the main concerns for unauthorized access was theft of property, product, and equipment. Theft has not grown; in fact, it has probably diminished. Now, other concerns such as the protection of company information, the security of employees, drug use, domestic violence in the workplace, disgruntled customers, ex- or current employees, and premises liability all make access control more important.

The major risks associated with the building perimeter are

- Uncontrolled access points;
- Too many potential access points;
- Recesses or obstructions may provide hiding places for intruders;
- Assault, robbery, and harassment of employees; and
- Vandalism and sabotage.

2.3.3 Building Services

This area includes cleaning, utility, and other equipment, systems, and services such as the following:

- Electrical
- Plumbing
- Water
- Boilers and furnaces
- Mechanical rooms
- Elevators
- Gas mains
- Heating, ventilation, and air conditioning
- Phone and computer services

The largest risk to the building services area is associated with the accidental or intentional disruption of service. Disruptions result in a risk to employee safety and the potential for the site to lose its ability to operate. This includes the following:

- Loss of service
- Interrupted service
- Personnel safety
- Product quality
- Losses due to theft of service and unauthorized use of communication systems

In this area, the risks most often relate to situations that involve the following:

- Construction, both planned or emergency
- Maintenance or service personnel (usually accidental)
- Disgruntled or destructive ex-employees, contractors, or vendors. These people are the most capable of doing substantial damage. Usually the acts are intentional.
- Injury to unauthorized personnel who have gained physical access to these areas.

2.3.4 Cafeteria

The risks most often associated with this area are

- Cash theft;
- Food, materials, and equipment theft;

- Vandalism;
- Contamination; and
- Shipping and receiving thefts.

2.3.5 Cash Handling and Cash Services

This area includes the cashier's area of a cafeteria, store, bar, or other retail operation. The risks for this area include:

- Robbery and employee injury;
- Theft, embezzlement, check kiting, and credit card fraud;
- Over-, under-, and no-ringing of merchandise; and
- Improper procedures for cash movements and bank deposits.

See the definition of *Zone 4* in Chapter 1 for more information about a higher-risk area located within a lower-risk one.

2.3.6 Chemicals: Transportation and Storage

The risks for this area include:

- Accidental or intentional release or spill;
- Accidental or intentional contamination;
- Damage to the company's reputation and image;
- Personal injury to employees, visitors, or uninvited guests;
- Lack of emergency procedures; and
- Unauthorized and inappropriate disposal.

2.3.7 Communications Equipment, Services, and Rooms

This area includes all aspects of your communications system, your phone equipment, phone service, phone room, and all aspects of any telecommunications system you may have.

Communications systems have always been a primary target for sabotage. Loss of communications, through either intentional or accidental events, can severely hamper your business.

The risks most often associated with this area can be divided into three main categories:

2.3.7.1 Equipment

- Accidental or intentional damage resulting in business interruption
- Loss or theft of equipment

2.3.7.2 Service

- Service interruption resulting in dissatisfied customers or lost customers
- Financial loss due to unauthorized use or theft of service—phone hackers are a new risk to communications systems
- Interception of proprietary information
- Lack of passwords or inappropriate passwords (access control)
- Illegal interception of communications

2.3.7.3 Room

- Physical damage, either intentional or accidental, to the equipment or service
- Unauthorized changes to system configuration

2.3.8 Computer Rooms and Services

Risks for this area include the following:

- Unauthorized access to your organization's networks and/or circumventing firewalls
- Illegal duplication of software
- Modification of data or software
- Theft of software or hardware
- Accidental or intentional damage resulting in business interruption
- Theft of proprietary information
- Illegal interception of communications
- Unauthorized use of computer services
- Accidental or intentional importation of viruses

2.3.9 Construction Sites

Construction sites include both large-scale construction and small, remodeling projects. Risks for this area include the following:

- Loss of proprietary information
- Accidental injury or damage to equipment
- Theft of company property
- Theft of personal property
- Sabotage
- Company liability
- Unauthorized equipment use
- Employee assaults
- Vehicle accidents

- Vandalism
- Billing fraud, timecard fraud
- Comingling of funds, equipment use, or materials use

2.3.10 Elevators
Risks for this area include the following:

- Accidents
- Personal security: assaults, robbery, harassment, and theft
- Unauthorized access to facilities, information, and people

2.3.11 Employee Store
Risks for this area include the following:

- Unauthorized or inappropriate access to your organization's facilities
- Unnecessary exposure to safety and security risks
- Product or property loss
- Loss of sales
- Threats to personal safety
- Loss of proprietary information
- Sabotage
- Damage to the company's reputation
- Legal concerns and issues of liability
- Accidental injury

2.3.12 Entrances and Exits
Controlling your facility's entrances and exits is the single most critical aspect of providing a secure work environment. Every form of security hinges on controlling access, especially physical access.

The risks that can be reduced by effectively limiting and controlling entrances and exits are

- Threats to personal safety;
- Loss of property, equipment, and product;
- Loss of proprietary information;
- Sabotage;
- Damage to the company's reputation;
- Legal concerns and issues of liability; and
- Accidental injury.

2.3.13 Executive Offices
This is often a Zone 4 area, with risks that include the following:

• Theft or access to proprietary or sensitive information
• Personal harm from internal or external persons

2.3.14 File Rooms
Security risks to the information stored in file rooms include those relating to unauthorized access of

• Proprietary information, such as product research or process methodology;
• Employee files; and
• Sales, marketing, pricing, and customer information.

As well as the physical risks to the actual files:

• Damage due to fire or water
• Theft or accidental loss of the files

2.3.15 Information Security
The most common risks to information security are

• Unauthorized access to restricted areas and proprietary information;
• Controlling disposal of waste; and
• Intelligence gathering by competitors.

2.3.16 Legal Concerns
The risks in this area include the following:

• Insufficient lighting
• Inadequate locks
• Lack of signs or improper signs
• Hazardous materials
• Dangerous traffic flow
• Vacant properties
• Attractive nuisances, such as lakes, ponds, towers, playgrounds, and equipment

2.3.17 Locker Areas
The risks to this area include the following:

• Protection of personal and company property

- Inappropriate use, storage, or concealment of contraband items (weapons, drugs, alcohol, etc.)
- Controlling access and privacy
- Effective separation between female and male locker areas

Note: Investigations of inappropriate activities in locker areas and restrooms are governed by extensive legal and human resource guidelines. No investigative or control efforts in these areas should be undertaken prior to consulting with your organization's corporate security and/or legal representatives.

2.3.18 Manufacturing Systems
The risks to this area include the following:

- Theft or access to proprietary or sensitive information
- Accidental or intentional release or spill
- Accidental or intentional contamination
- Damage to company's reputation and image
- Personal injury to employees, visitors, or uninvited guests
- Lack of emergency procedures

2.3.19 Miscellaneous Areas, Temporary Conditions, Special Situations, and Other Areas that Require Additional Precautions
Sometimes there are other areas and special situations that require additional precautions. Although the operations in these areas must be controlled, it is not always possible to locate the area inside the facility.

These areas require increased precautions due to civil liability regulations; for environmental reasons; or for safety, security, or aesthetic reasons. Some examples of these areas are as follows:

- Settling ponds
- Material storage areas
- Transformers
- Post indicator valves (PIV)
- Water and fuel tanks
- Chemical or supply tanks
- Salvage scrap areas
- Vehicle or trailer storage areas
- Power generation equipment

- Utilities and entrances to utilities
- HVAC
- Water systems
- Sewage systems
- Hazardous waste
- Air intake and exhaust systems
- Fire systems
- Fuel (gas, propane, diesel, oil)
- Electrical service
- Telephone equipment rooms and service
- Telecommunications

The risks associated with these areas include the following:

- Children playing in the area
- Theft
- Sabotage by disgruntled or former employees, contractors, or vendors, or by social or political activists
- Contamination: either accidental or intentional
- Injury due to unauthorized use

2.3.20 Multiple Tenant Facilities

Sharing office space, warehouse space, or manufacturing facilities with other operations or with your organization's operations that have different security needs often creates security risks:

- Sharing facility access and common areas, such as restrooms, parking, cafeterias, vertical exit stair towers, elevators, and loading docks puts your organization's people in contact with others who are potentially interested in compromising your organization's security.
- The facility managers or owners may not support security measures.
- Unless you are careful to negotiate access control issues prior to signing a contract and taking occupancy, you may have no control over common access points to the facility or service areas.

2.3.21 Multiple Use/Public Space Areas

Spaces or areas within the facility designed for use by both employees and visitors are called multiple use areas or general areas.

Risks to these areas include the following:

- Access to other more restricted areas can often be gained from multiple use areas
- Accidental exposure to proprietary information: the most likely risk is associated with discussions of proprietary information in the presence of unauthorized personnel

2.3.22 Office Equipment

The risks in this area pertain to loss of equipment, loss of use, and unauthorized use.

- Theft
- Vandalism
- Illegal or inappropriate use

2.3.23 Open Space/Rental Property/Building Grounds

This area includes all your organization's property in the following categories: vacant land, land acquisitions, vacant or unoccupied buildings, staging areas, unused parking lots, lawns, pallet and drum storage areas, tank farms, and containment areas.

Use your organization's security performance guidelines to reduce risks to this area, which include the following:

- Walk-in or uninvited guests
- Unauthorized parking, drinking, or gathering by employees or non-employees
- Public use of the space as a shortcut, or for off-road vehicles
- Driver training or bicycle riding
- Unwanted animals
- Illegal dumping of wastes, garbage, or vehicles

2.3.24 Outdoor Areas for Employees

Areas such as walking paths, picnic areas, baseball fields, softball fields, tennis courts, golf courses, shooting ranges, hiking trails, playgrounds, lodges, boating areas, hangers, and other recreational areas are all included in this category. Due to a variety of factors, outdoor employee areas are becoming a greater source of security concern:

- These areas are much more common (many facilities now include such areas).

- They are often a weak point for access control. There is no easy way to control entry and egress.
- Personal safety is lower, due to non-supervision and isolation. There usually is no full-time staffing of these areas.
- Guests and family members often use this area.
- Property and/or products are easy to remove.
- Personal property is usually allowed in these areas.
- These areas are attractive to outsiders and uninvited guests. There is likely to be some level of unauthorized use.

2.3.25 Parking Areas

Parking areas have a very high volume of routine activity; consequently, they provide a host of security-related concerns. Parking issues can affect everything from employee morale to personal safety to company liability. The risks for this area include the following:

- Pedestrian accidents
- Traffic accidents
- Vandalism
- Hit-and-run property damage
- Drug and alcohol, use and sales
- Harassment from non-employees
- Assaults
- Robbery
- Storage of prohibited items, such as guns, alcohol, and drugs

2.3.26 Personnel Security

The risks faced by the people who work at your facility go beyond the perimeters of the work site. The risks include the following:

- Traveling safely to and from work
- Risks associated with traveling out of town
- Vehicle security at work and at home
- Parking lot thefts and assaults
- Crime and domestic violence coming into the workplace
- Former employees, vendors, and contractors as a risk to employee safety
- Security of family members and/or homes while employees are at work

The security of the people who work at your facility can be significantly enhanced by following these personnel security guidelines:

* Encourage people to use the security measures that are available.
* Install and maintain lighting that meets your organization's engineering standards.
* Use escort services, or walk with someone else whenever possible.
* Lock doors and offices whenever possible.
* If you are working after dark, and you are visible from outside the building, use blinds or drapery to block a direct view from the exterior.
* Provide a duress alarm system in work environments for which it is appropriate.
* Provide peephole hardware to enhance solid doors.

2.3.27 Phone Equipment Room
The phone equipment room has always been a very common target for sabotage. Loss of your phone system, through intentional or accidental events, can severely hamper your business. Physical security as well as systems configuration are essential to phone system security.

Risks to this area include the following:

* Phone hackers
* Loss of information
* Financial loss due to unauthorized use
* Loss of business and customer dissatisfaction

2.3.28 Proprietary Production Areas
Risks to this area include the following:

* Theft of trade secrets
* Accidental or intentional damage
* Business interruption

See *Zone 4* later in this section for more information.

2.3.29 Public Phones and Restrooms
Risks to this area include the following:

* Phone crimes and frauds
* Personnel safety
* Dollar losses due to unauthorized use

- Loss of company's reputation and public image can be the result of inappropriate use of your organization's phones or property

See *Multiple Tenant Facilities* earlier in this section for more information.

2.3.30 Public Safety/Emergency Response
Risks to this area include the following:

- Inappropriate emergency response to hazardous chemicals, contamination, wastes, and spills; to criminal incidents; to natural disasters, fires, and explosions; and to equipment failures, construction, and operational accidents
- Legal risks due to inappropriate response
- Response failure due to inadequate notification and communication
- Lack of signs or inappropriate signs
- Equipment that is missing or non-functioning
- Lack of emergency vehicle access, or blocked access due to inappropriate parking controls or temporary construction

2.3.31 Raw Materials Areas
Risks to this area include the following:

- Theft
- Sabotage
- Inventory inaccuracy
- Loss of use

2.3.32 Reception Areas
Risks to this area include the following:

- Inadequate screening of visitors and employees prior to their admittance to non-public areas
- Protecting sensitive information (such as mail, messages, documents, and work in progress) in a public area
- Reception personnel untrained in emergency procedures and notification leading to inappropriate responses

2.3.33 Research and Development Areas
Risks to this area include the following:

- Loss of information, process, or procedures

- Accidental or intentional damage to experiments or tests
- Injury to uninvited guests
- Damage to the company's reputation

See *Zone 4* later in this section for more information.

2.3.34 Roof Openings
Risks to this area include the following:

- Unauthorized access to the facility
- Inappropriate access to roof by untrained or unauthorized personnel
- Exposure to roof emissions

2.3.35 Sales and Marketing
Risks to this area include the following:

- Personnel security: on the road, in hotels, at customs, in vehicles and aircraft, and on the street
- Information security: pricing, volume, customer and account information
- Computer security in cars and in airports
- Security of offices in the home: destruction or loss of information

2.3.36 Scrap and Salvage
Risks to this area include the following:

- Financial loss from loss of sales
- Environmental issues arising from improper or illegal disposal
- Pricing and market disruption, if diverted to the marketplace or sold
- Fraud and collusion
- Damage to the company's reputation
- Product warranty, replacement claims, and liability issues relating to products that have been diverted back into the market

2.3.37 Sensitive Parts Storage
Risks to this area include the following:

- Loss, either accidental or deliberate
- Loss of proprietary information
- Reduced productivity, if a required part is not available

See *Zone 4* later in this section for more information.

2.3.38 Shipping and Receiving and Postage/Mailroom Areas

Shipping and receiving areas are used by many people who are not your organization's employees. This leads to increased risks in the following areas:

- Personal safety
- Loss of property, equipment, and product
- Loss of information
- Inappropriate use of postage and mail shipping facilities
- Legal liabilities
- Potential unauthorized access to the facility beyond; controlled access is recommended

Close control of these areas is required to keep risks within acceptable levels.

2.3.39 Supply Rooms

Risks to this area include the following:

- Use of supplies by unauthorized personnel or the unauthorized use of those supplies by personnel who do have legitimate access to supplies
- Waste
- Sabotage
- Purchasing fraud

2.3.40 Tool Rooms

Risks to this area include the following:

- Loss of tools and equipment
- Use by unauthorized personnel such as contractors and vendors
- Injury due to use of tools by untrained personnel

See *Zone 4* later in this section for more information.

2.3.41 Vaults

Risks to this area include the following:

- Loss of valuable property
- Key codes or combination codes loss, loss of accountability for these codes

- Loss of personnel responsibility and accountability due to uncontrolled access

See *Zone 4* later in this section for more information.

2.3.42 Warehouse
Risks to this area include the following:

- Collusion with drivers or "will call" for thefts
- Theft
- Personal use of Fedex or UPS services
- Sabotage
- Loss of goods due to fire or water damage
- Loss of goods due to poor accountability in the returned goods area or the claims area
- Contamination of products
- Loss of company reputation and good will from damaged products being delivered to customer
- Potential unauthorized access to the facility beyond; controlled access is recommended

See *Shipping and Receiving* earlier in this section for more information.

2.3.43 Windows
Generally speaking, windows are a weak point in the perimeter. Risks to this area include the following:

- Ease of unauthorized access to an area
- Visual access, auditory access, and physical access can be gained to an area
- Loss of proprietary processing information

2.3.44 Zone 4
Zone 4 areas are those restricted areas of your business that often require additional security beyond that which is normally provided for your business. Risks to this area include the following:

- Loss of high value property, product, information, or technology
- Interruption of operations, resulting in significant loss
- Loss of personnel or customers that negatively affect business operations

- Loss of product lead time, market share, or profitability
- Damage to your organization's ability to attract and keep good employees

Note: The above Zone 4 risks are associated with theft, damage, destruction, disclosure, and loss of use of any equipment, products, processes, technology, or human resources in a restricted area.

CHAPTER 3

Security Performance Guidelines and Options

3.1 INTRODUCTION

This chapter discusses the security performance guidelines and options relevant to each functional area of your business. These guidelines and options are meant to help you take action after you have reviewed the security risks to a particular area and have decided that the area does not have the appropriate level of security.

The functional areas in this chapter are arranged alphabetically, as in the previous chapter. For each area, the following information is given:

- Planning considerations
- Suggested minimum security requirements
- Recommended enhancements

Note: In this chapter, the suggested minimum security requirements for an area are indicated by a single check mark (✓). Recommended enhancements, on the other hand, are indicated by a double check mark (✓✓).

The security measures or options given for a specific area are designed to bring that area up to its appropriate level of security. The particular option you select depends on your facility and your business operations. In some cases, the suggested minimum requirements may be the best way to meet an area's security needs. The overall goal is to maintain a level of security that is most appropriate for each area of your business.

3.1.1 Performance Guidelines

In Chapter 1, we introduced the eight security performance guidelines that you need to be aware of (see Figure 3.1). These guidelines are the security goals for your organization's business operation and site.

Performance Guidelines	
1. Identify your security needs	5. Detect unauthorized access
2. Integrate security	6. Be prepared for an incident
3. Control physical access	7. Respond effectively
4. Control information access	8. Report promptly

Figure 3.1 Performance Guidelines.

3.2 FUNCTIONAL AREAS: GUIDELINES AND OPTIONS

The functional areas of your business are listed, in alphabetic order, in the following sections.[1] For each area, the following information is given:

- Planning considerations
- Suggested minimum security requirements (✓)
- Recommended enhancements (✓✓)

Keep in mind: a planning consideration that is common to every functional area included in this chapter is to review the performance guidelines in Figure 3.1 and apply them appropriately.

3.2.1 Access Control for Property and Undeveloped Land

Planning Considerations

- Review your access control policy. Ensure compliance with your organization's access control and ID policy (see Chapter 1).
- What are the realistic types of threat to the facility?
- Assess the volume and composition of pedestrian traffic in the area.
- Will signs and clear perimeter lines control pedestrian walk-on?
- Do you need barriers, gates, fences, or berms to control access and circulation?
- How do visitors access the site? Do they need a separate access point?
- Is adequate parking provided in appropriate locations?
- Is it possible to light the site effectively?

---

[1] If you want to review the kinds of security risks associated with each area, please refer back to Chapter 2.

Suggested Minimum Security Requirements

✓ Use an environmental design that incorporates natural barriers and landscaping.
✓ Install signs of the right type in the right places to show the extent of your organization's property, the circulation pattern in effect, and any potential hazards on the property.
✓ Use lighting that conforms to national lighting standards.
✓ Minimize access and egress points.
✓ Use walkways, tunnels, and overpasses to avoid additional access points.
✓ If fencing is used, secure or control access to all gates.
✓ Perform routine inspections and provide an audit trail of all inspections.
✓ Be certain that you have the rights to inspect property and vehicles by posting the required signs.
✓ Park trucks, forklifts, and other vehicles away from fences and buildings so as to not provide assistance to those seeking unauthorized access to the facility. Be certain to remove the keys from all vehicles.

Recommended Enhancements

✓✓ Utilize electronic access control systems in conjunction with human oversight and involvement.
✓✓ Provide intrusion and unauthorized egress detection systems.

3.2.2 Access Control for a Site that is a Functioning Business Operation

Planning Considerations

• Review your access control policy. Ensure compliance with your organization's access control and ID policy (see Chapter 1).
• What are the realistic types of threat to the facility?
• Assess the volume and composition of pedestrian traffic in the area.
• Will signs and clear perimeter lines control pedestrian walk-on?
• Is it sufficient to have a set of restricted vehicle access points?
• Do you need barriers, gates, fences, or berms to control access and circulation?
• How do visitors access the site? Do they need a separate access point?
• Is adequate parking provided in appropriate locations?
• Is it possible to light the site effectively?

Suggested Minimum Security Requirements

✓ Use an environmental design that incorporates natural barriers and landscaping.
✓ Install signs of the right type in the right places to show the extent of your organization's property, the circulation pattern in effect, and any potential hazards on the property.
✓ Use lighting that conforms to national lighting standards
✓ Minimize access and egress points.
✓ Use walkways, tunnels, and overpasses to avoid additional access points.
✓ If fencing is used, secure or control access to all gates.
✓ Perform routine inspections and provide an audit trail of all inspections.
✓ Be certain that you have the rights to inspect property and vehicles by posting the required signs.
✓ Park trucks, forklifts, and other vehicles away from fences and buildings so as to not provide assistance to those seeking unauthorized access to the facility. Be certain to remove the keys from all vehicles.

Recommended Enhancements

✓✓ Utilize electronic access control systems in conjunction with human oversight and involvement.
✓✓ Provide intrusion and unauthorized egress detection systems.

3.2.3 Access Control for a Building or Part of a Building (see also Multiple Tenant Facilities)

Planning Considerations

- Review your access control policy. Ensure compliance with your organization's access control and ID policy (see Chapter 1).
- Not only must the perimeter be secured against unauthorized persons, it must also be secured against authorized persons gaining access at the wrong time or for the wrong reason.
- New business trends, such as the use of contract employees, contract manufacturing, and contracted services such as cleaning and trucking, produce a higher volume of individuals who are inside the facility. In addition, all these people have an extended group of friends, family, and other employees who know something about your site and who can test your security system.

- Integrate policies, procedures, and human intervention with technology to provide a secure building perimeter.
- The more openings in the building, the more difficult it is to control access.
- Do the number of access points meet the access requirements of the business? Are there too many?
- Where do visitors, employees, contractors, and service personnel enter the building?
- Are building, shipping, and receiving access points separated?
- Are the access points properly lighted to meet engineering's lighting standards?

Suggested Minimum Security Requirements

✓ Use an environmental design that incorporates natural barriers and landscaping.
✓ Install signs of the right type in the right places to show the extent of your organization's property, the circulation pattern in effect, and any potential hazards on the property.
✓ Use lighting that conforms to national lighting standards
✓ Minimize access and egress points.
✓ Provide intrusion and unauthorized egress detection systems.
✓ Use walkways, tunnels, and overpasses to avoid additional access points.
✓ If fencing is used, secure or control access to all gates.
✓ Perform routine inspections and provide an audit trail of all inspections.
✓ Be certain that you have the rights to inspect property and vehicles by posting the required signs.
✓ Park trucks, forklifts, and other vehicles away from fences and buildings so as to not provide assistance to those seeking unauthorized access to the facility. Be certain to remove the keys from all vehicles.
✓ Secure doors and windows against unauthorized entry and egress.
✓ Secure utility access points and other structures near a building to prevent their use for unauthorized entry.

Recommended Enhancements

✓✓ Use electronic access control systems in conjunction with human oversight and involvement.

✓✓ Provide CCTV camera and recording coverage at primary entry and egress points.

✓✓ Use an alarm system to annunciate unauthorized access and egress.

3.2.4 Building Services

Planning Considerations

- Control access and provide an audit trail to reduce the risks associated with the area.
- Minimize the number of entry points.
- Make an assessment of both the company and personnel providing the service and the degree of security necessary for meeting the performance guidelines.
- Consider the time of day the service is provided and the amount of supervision required when screening potential service vendors.
- Develop a contingency plan for dealing with a loss of service.

Suggested Minimum Security Requirements

✓ Use a list of preapproved personnel from the company providing the service.

✓ Establish and maintain procedures that keep current the list(s) of authorized personnel.

✓ Use locks and locking hardware, key control, and an audit trail for the area accessed by the service personnel.

✓ Post clear and obvious signs for restricted access and hazardous areas.

✓ Assign security responsibility to a single individual for each critical service.

Recommended Enhancements

✓✓ Restrict access to only those areas and times required for completion of installation, maintenance, and upgrade work.

✓✓ Use electronic access systems for areas with high personnel volumes or high personnel turnover.

✓✓ Use intrusion devices for areas that exceed safe levels of vulnerability or criticality.

3.2.5 Cafeteria

Planning Considerations

- It is critical that cafeterias are located within public areas of your facility. See *Public Spaces* in this chapter and *Adjacency Planning* in Chapter 1 for more information about planning for areas that contain or connect to public areas.
- The cafeteria's design should provide for a one-way flow of traffic from food selection to cashier.
- Provide an inventory storage space that has controlled and monitored access.
- There must be a safe or other secure container for storing receipts, or a bank-deposit procedure to eliminate cash security problems.

Suggested Minimum Security Requirements

- ✓ Control access to the dining areas if they provide access to an area that is not open to the public.
- ✓ Secure kitchen areas and stores during non-operational hours with a locking hardware system.
- ✓ Hold security reviews on contracted food services, both the contract employees and the contract itself.
- ✓ Provide for secure cash storage.
- ✓ Clearly sign areas that have restricted access or are hazardous.

Recommended Enhancements

- ✓✓ Use an electronic access control system where appropriate.

3.2.6 Cash Handling

Planning Considerations

- If the cash handling area is to be used by both employees and non-employees, locate the area in a public space. See *Public Spaces* for more information.
- Plan for secure cash storage and for low-risk cash transit.
- Review cash processing procedures so as to limit personnel involvement and minimize errors. Automate the process by using bar code scanning, payroll deductions, and other management techniques that remove cash from the system.

- Review your policies and procedures with internal auditing.
- If cash handling or cash storage amounts exceed $1,000, plan for intrusion and theft alarm systems.

Suggested Minimum Security Requirements

✓ Control access to the cash storage and cash processing areas such as cash rooms, cash machines, and storage containers.
✓ Use preemployment screening of all persons who will have responsibility for cash transactions and processing.
✓ Review your cash policies and procedures with internal auditing on a regular basis.
✓ Use locks and locking hardware, with key control and audit trails, to secure cash areas.

Recommended Enhancements

✓✓ For cash handling and storage areas that have amounts in excess of $1,000, install an alarm system that monitors and annunciates alarm conditions. See *Alarms Systems* in Chapter 4 for more information.
✓✓ Use recorded CCTV to monitor activity.

3.2.7 Chemicals

Planning Considerations

- Ensure that a review is conducted with the appropriate technical personnel so that the risks to this area are identified and minimized.
- Design the area to control access and contain spills.
- Develop operational procedures that establish adequate controls.
- Train your personnel and local emergency response units.

Suggested Minimum Security Requirements

✓ Use barriers to secure the areas where chemicals are stored.
✓ Post signs on all chemical storage areas.

Recommended Enhancements

✓✓ Use electronic access control systems.
✓✓ Install equipment that detects unauthorized access and that provides early warning/notification of releases or spills.

✓✓ Provide recorded CCTV to monitor access control points and other appropriate activity in the area.

3.2.8 Communications Equipment, Services, and Rooms

Planning Considerations

- Depending on your business, loss of phone service can be anything from an inconvenience to a devastating setback. Assess the criticality of phone service to your business and structure your security measures accordingly.
- Have in place procedures for temporary replacement of telephone services in case your system fails.
- Schedule phone system service, repairs, and upgrades during business hours whenever possible. Provide escorts for the service personnel.
- During the design phase, be certain to locate the telecommunication rooms away from areas where proprietary information or processes may inadvertently be exposed.
- Telecommunications areas are part of an interior concentric zone of protection, probably Zone 4, where only those people with a demonstrated business need are given authorized access.
- Doors, locking hardware, and construction must be designed to delay unauthorized access, allow for detection, and promote quick response.
- Plan for adequate environmental equipment such as uninterruptable power, heating, cooling, and humidity controls.
- Plan for access and audit controls that ensure preapproved, authorized nonemployees working in the area have an appropriate level of supervision.

Suggested Minimum Security Requirements

✓ Configure systems in accordance with IT, telecommunications, and your organization's security representative recommendations.
✓ Clearly sign areas of restricted access and hazardous areas.
✓ Control access to all interior equipment and provide an audit trail of access to the area.
✓ Escort visitors and employees as appropriate.
✓ Maintain an audit trail of all access activity into the area.
✓ Control access to all exterior equipment such as satellite ground stations, microwave parabolic reflectors, and communications towers/supports.

✓ Ensure that online information, passwords, and procedural controls are at a level consistent with the physical access controls.
✓ Develop operational security procedures in accordance with IT security's systems guidelines.

Recommended Enhancements

✓✓ Install recorded CCTV with video monitor and time/day/date recording capability to monitor the area and entrance(s) to the area.
✓✓ Use an alarm monitoring system. Provide for local response to alarms.
✓✓ Use electronic card access where appropriate.
✓✓ Control access to all interior spaces and equipment with remote management services (RMS) and CCTV and provide an electronic audit trail.

3.2.9 Computer Rooms

Planning Considerations

- Computer rooms are part of an interior concentric zone of protection, probably Zone 4, where only those people with a demonstrated business need are given authorized access.
- Prior to the purchase of security hardware and software, an evaluation of the security design features must be completed in conjunction with IT, telecommunications, and your organization's security representative.
- Doors, locking hardware, and construction must be designed to delay unauthorized access, allow for detection, and promote quick response.
- It may be critical that you have procedures in place for temporary replacement of computer services if your system fails.
- Plan for adequate environmental equipment such as uninterruptable power, heating, cooling, and humidity controls.
- Provide access procedures and audit controls that ensure pre-approved authorized nonemployees working in the area have an appropriate level of supervision.
- Ensure that online information, passwords, and procedural controls are at a level consistent with the physical access controls.
- All operational security procedures must be in accordance with IT security systems guidelines.

Suggested Minimum Security Requirements

✓ Configure systems in accordance with IT, telecommunications, and your organization's security recommendations.
✓ Clearly sign areas of restricted access and hazardous areas.
✓ Control access to all interior equipment and provide an audit trail of all access to the area.
✓ Escort visitors and employees as appropriate.
✓ Use locks and locking hardware, along with the appropriate key control and audit trail procedures.

Recommended Enhancements

✓✓ Install recorded CCTV with video monitor and time/day/date recording capability to monitor the area.
✓✓ Use an alarm monitoring system. Provide for local response to alarms.
✓✓ Use electronic card access where appropriate.
✓✓ Control access to all interior spaces and equipment with RMS and CCTV and provide an electronic audit trail.
✓✓ Maintain an audit trail of all access activity into the area, during both business and non-business hours.

3.2.10 Construction Sites

Planning Considerations

• Determine how to define construction areas and how to segregate them from existing organization property and facilities.
• Limit entry and exit points.
• Plan for adequate lighting in compliance with national lighting standards.
• Plan for and design access control credentials and follow your organization's access control and ID policy (see Chapter 1).
• Define material, tool, and equipment requirements.
• Integrate control procedures for materials, tools, and equipment with existing operations.
• Plan for construction personnel parking. Minimize unnecessary vehicle entry/exit activity.

Suggested Minimum Security Requirements

✓ Provide temporary fencing.
✓ Provide a locking system that is keyed independently until the project is complete. Rekey the system so that it meets your organization's requirements at the time of your organization's acceptance and occupancy.
✓ Construction and service personnel must be trained in the site's safety and security requirements and procedures.

Recommended Enhancements

✓✓ Use a recorded CCTV system to monitor activity.
✓✓ Provide security patrols.
✓✓ Designate an organization security officer, organization employee, or contract security officer to control access and patrol the area.

3.2.11 Data Storage

Planning Considerations

- Physically locate on-site data storage areas as far away from IT (or information services) as possible.
- Plan for off-site storage, depending on the value, amount, and criticality of the data.
- Review your facilities for protection against the natural hazards appropriate for your geographic location (e.g., floods, earthquakes, tornadoes).
- Review your facilities and your security measures for protection against accidental damage due to fire, explosion, and structural collapse.
- Review your security measures to protect against human damage, both intentional and accidental (e.g., theft, destruction, tampering or modification, chemical spills).

Suggested Minimum Security Requirements

✓ Control access to minimize the number of people who access the area.
✓ Provide an audit trail of all access activity.
✓ Use smart locking systems, with key control or unique individual PINs providing audit trail.

✓ Design data storage containers specifically for protection against fire, theft, water damage, spills, and tampering.

Recommended Enhancements

✓✓ Use alarms systems with local annunciation and response.
✓✓ Use recorded CCTV to monitor activity.

3.2.12 Elevators

Planning Considerations

- Control access to elevator equipment rooms.
- Integrate elevator systems with security monitoring systems.
- Plan for controlled access where appropriate.
- Locate the elevator towers within the interior of the facility, preferably within a Zone 3 element.
- Plan to accommodate controlled public access.
- Isolate sensitive business areas away from elevators and their traffic patterns.

Suggested Minimum Security Requirements

✓ Control access during non-business hours when appropriate.
✓ Monitor for alarm conditions.
✓ Equip all elevators with emergency lighting and communications equipment.
✓ If your organization shares occupancy of a building with other businesses, maintain the necessary level of security through an access control system at a point before your organization's space is entered.

Recommended Enhancements

✓✓ Use electronic access control systems.
✓✓ Use recorded CCTV to monitor the elevators.
✓✓ If you want to use a keypad access control system, do not use a common code. Smart keypads with unique PINs or cards offer a more secure system.

3.2.13 Employee Store

Planning Considerations

- Plan for cash handling and cash holding areas.

- To protect inventory, plan for controlled access during non-business hours.
- Select a location next to or within a public space to restrict access to your organization's business space and operations.
- Provide direct access from the store to public facilities (restrooms, telephones, water fountains, vending machines, etc.)
- Review floor plan for customer traffic flow that's appropriate for the store's hours, location, and sales volume.
- If cash handling and storage exceed $1,000, plan for intrusion and theft alarm systems.

Suggested Minimum Security Requirements

✓ Post signs for personal use/no resale products, maximum quantity allowed, escort policy, restricted areas, and other information the customers need to know.
✓ Control after-hours access and provide an audit trail.
✓ Provide employees with training on cash handling, robbery, and theft procedures.
✓ Establish purchase records and log the frequency of restricted sale merchandise purchased by each customer.
✓ Place high-value, high-risk items in locations that will minimize shoplifting.
✓ Review cash handling and balancing procedures with internal audits for appropriate controls.
✓ Provide locking hardware and key control for the entrances and exits.

Recommended Enhancements

✓✓ Install recorded CCTV to monitor activity.
✓✓ Use electronic access systems for appropriate areas.

3.2.14 Entrances and Exits

Planning Considerations

- Your ability to control your building's entrances and exits depends on your access control methods. The probability of security incidents or losses resulting from unauthorized persons gaining access to a facility is greatly reduced by well-designed and frequently validated access control methods. In addition, your methods must allow you to handle exceptions and to escalate security measures rapidly when necessary.

- Plan for alarm response. Your organization's policy should require controlled access and an audit trail.
- Design a limited number of active entrances and exits into the plan for your facility.
- In the design of an entrance, anticipate the peak periods of traffic and control.
- At facilities with 200 or more employees, consider separate entrances for visitors, employees, and services, to avoid conflicts in circulation and in access control.
- At manufacturing and distribution sites, consider separate and controlled entrances for shipping, receiving, and warehousing functions
- All exit-only doors must be used solely for exiting.
- Plan for integration of equipment and personnel to reduce costs and increase effectiveness.

Suggested Minimum Security Requirements

- ✓ Control access in accordance with your organization's policy.
- ✓ Use a badging system to meet access control requirements for both employees and nonemployees.
- ✓ Provide smart locking systems with key control and audit trail.
- ✓ Secure doors and post signs as necessary.
- ✓ Provide lighting in accordance with national lighting standards
- ✓ Use door seals or emergency exit alarms on exit-only doors.
- ✓ Escort visitors when appropriate. See Chapter 4, *Escort Policy*, for more information.
- ✓ Post clear signs at vehicle and pedestrian entrances and exits.
- ✓ To reduce the risk of unauthorized access, and to lower the costs of door hardware, eliminate exterior hardware from exit-only doors whenever possible.
- ✓ Review your procedures and inspect all entrances and exits frequently. Be certain to validate that all equipment, systems, and services are operating as designed.

Recommended Enhancements

- ✓✓ Provide recorded CCTV to monitor all access activity.
- ✓✓ Use electronic access control systems where appropriate.

3.2.15 Executive Offices and Spaces

Planning Considerations

- Plan for the ability to increase security controls to emergency levels in times of threatened, attempted, or actual incidents of physical harm, property loss, or information loss.
- Plan for the ability to positively identify all persons requesting access to the area.
- Locate the area away from public access and direct employee access.
- Plan for parking facilities and security that are consistent with executive office security measures.
- Plan transparent and convenient security measures for both business and nonbusiness hours.

Suggested Minimum Security Requirements

- ✓ Use smart locking hardware and key control.
- ✓ Control access during after-business hours.
- ✓ Prescreen visitors and guests.
- ✓ Install a duress alarm system.
- ✓ Use recorded CCTV to monitor access activity.
- ✓ Use alarm systems integrated with security response.
- ✓ Post the appropriate signs.
- ✓ Secure office equipment and furniture consistent with sensitive information and proprietary property.
- ✓ Secure stairwells consistent with access controls throughout the executive areas.

Recommended Enhancements

- ✓✓ Use electronic access control systems.

3.2.16 File Rooms

Planning Considerations

- Design file rooms to detect and stop unauthorized access.
- Plan for the physical protection of file storage equipment and materials from fire, smoke, water, and other physical damage.

Suggested Minimum Security Requirements

✓ Implement procedures that control access to the file rooms and to the files themselves.
✓ Use smart locking systems, with strict key control.
✓ Maintain an audit trail of all access to the file rooms during non-business hours.
✓ Keep all cabinets and storage areas locked during non-business hours.

Recommended Enhancements

✓✓ Use electronic access control systems that supplement the access control procedures.
✓✓ Use intrusion detection devices and maintain an audit trail of all activity.

3.2.17 Locker Facilities

Planning Considerations

• Design locker locations so that they are only accessible by authorized personnel.
• Separate men's and women's facilities and the traffic patterns that correspond to the use of the facilities.
• Be certain that the facilities do not have a direct entry to or exit from the building or the property without passing a control point.

Suggested Minimum Security Requirements

✓ When lockers are required, the lockers and locking hardware must be provided by management.
✓ Maintain a register of occupancy.
✓ Locking hardware must incorporate a master keying or combination locking system, which has been provided and maintained by management.

3.2.18 Manufacturing Systems

Planning Considerations

• Design system locations so that they are accessible to only authorized personnel.

- Design motor control centers and rack rooms as fire-rated rooms.

Suggested Minimum Security Requirements

✓ Control access to rooms housing control equipment.
✓ Maintain documentation in a secured location.
✓ Post signs consistent with inspection guidelines.

Recommended Enhancements

✓✓ Use smart-locking hardware and key control or use electronic access control systems that supplement the access control procedures.
✓✓ Use intrusion detection devices and maintain an audit trail of all activity.

3.2.19 Multiple Tenant Facilities

Planning Considerations

- Assess your cotenants as to the potential security risks associated with each of them, for example:
  - Circulation patterns for other tenants creates or transfers risks to your organization.
  - Political activists, religious activists, or other socially sensitive groups are targeting another tenant.
  - Another tenant is providing a high-risk product or a controversial service, such as medical or abortion services, research or production of nuclear materials, products with environmental impact, use of precious metals, or delivery of armored car service.
- Be certain that another tenant's hours of operation are not a risk to your organization.
- Separate and control, as much as possible, building services such as:
  - Parking
  - Restrooms
  - Storage areas
  - Utilities
  - Elevators
  - Entrances
  - Maintenance and cleaning services
  - Shipping and receiving
  - Waste disposal

- Security and alarm services
- Negotiate authorization to upgrade and operate security services to your organization's suggested minimum security requirements in access control, security or police response, locking systems, and control systems.
- Negotiate the authority to control access times and conditions of building management and service personnel to your organization's spaces.
- Building management and tenants should not have unaccounted for or unrestricted access to your organization's space and operations.
- Plan for access control needs that result from other tenants' circulation patterns, which relate to:
  - Elevators
  - Stair wells
  - Service corridors
  - Utilities
  - Emergency exits and corridors
- Plan for secure construction methods that separate and secure your organization's space to protect from all kinds of intrusion: audio, visual, and physical.
- Your organization should control and contract for its own security services. Employment standards for contractors of all kinds should be reviewed by your organization to ensure that the contractors are acceptable.
- Consult with your organization's security representative early during site selection, and conduct a security survey prior to lease negotiation or facility planning.

Suggested Minimum Security Requirements

✓ Use access control procedures that meet your organization's standards and are in accordance with your organization's policy.
✓ Use smart locking systems with key control.
✓ Post clear signs and notifications.
✓ Use lighting that meets your organization's engineering lighting standards.

Recommended Enhancements

✓✓ Use electronic access control systems.
✓✓ Use recorded CCTV to monitor activity.

3.2.20 Multiple use and Public Space Areas

Planning Considerations

- Whenever possible, plan for direct entry into these areas from the facility's main entrance or lobby area.
- If restrooms and public phones are within the multiple use area, visitors and other non-employees do not need to go beyond this area.
- During new construction or renovation, location selection is critical. The most cost-effective and procedurally effective way to reduce risk is through space and adjacency planning. Physical and procedural control can be very inconvenient and unacceptable in many areas; often these problems can only be eliminated by effective site selection and location.
- Meeting rooms where visitors and suppliers conduct business should be set up to reduce circulation patterns into the facility's interior.
- Do not allow direct access from multiple use areas to other areas in the facility without a control point.
- Shipping and receiving functions should be designed to eliminate the need for additional access controls and procedural controls.

Suggested Minimum Security Requirements

If the design layout does not eliminate the need for security controls beyond the perimeter access, then:

✓ Use your organization's badge and ID system to control access; and
✓ Implement escort procedures.

Under all conditions:

✓ Use smart locking hardware with key control and audit trail to secure the area, equipment, and inventory during non-business hours;
✓ Use physical controls for cash handling, movement, and storage;
✓ Provide secure and controlled-access storage areas for equipment and inventory; and
✓ Use intrusion alarms and monitoring.

3.2.21 Office Equipment

Planning Considerations

- Control of office equipment must be local—a department or area manager is usually the appropriate person to be assigned this responsibility.

- Where high-risk and critical equipment is used or stored, involve your organization's security representative in a formal risk assessment and in the design of appropriate security measures.
- The best way to reduce risk to office equipment is the consistent application of site access control procedures that are in accordance with your organization's policy.
- Minimize the number of points where material is received and removed.
- Place all office equipment on your fixed assets list.

Suggested Minimum Security Requirements

✓ Inventory all equipment and place it on the fixed assets list.
✓ Prevent unauthorized use of equipment.
✓ Control access in accordance with your organization's policy.
✓ Develop and use a proprietary pass system for equipment that may be removed from the area.
✓ Lock all desks, storage cabinets, and equipment when not in use and during non-business hours.
✓ Assign one person the responsibility for equipment movement and accountability.

Recommended Enhancements

✓✓ Attach high-risk or easy-to-move equipment such as scales and microscopes to the desk top or table top.
✓✓ Apply electronic equipment control systems where warranted. Electronic systems may be effective, but they should not be implemented before consulting with your organization's security representative.
✓✓ Office equipment, such as personal computers that may be transported to or used in homes, should have the same level of accountability and security in the home as when it is on your organization's property.
✓✓ In sites where after-hours access is authorized, but human intervention is not available, video recording is the only means available for establishing materials control and audit trails.

3.2.22 Open Space

Planning Considerations

- Prepare an effective risk assessment based on the risks identified in Chapter 2.

- In most situations, the appropriate signs and notifications regarding restricted use should be posted.
- Implement detection and inspection procedures to ensure that unauthorized situations are detected and reported.
- Take corrective action to prevent or respond to unauthorized use.

Suggested Minimum Security Requirements

✓ Use appropriate signs to identify your organization's property boundaries, to guide circulation and traffic patterns, to post use restriction notices, and to provide appropriate warnings for the site.
✓ Limit vegetation and remove visual obstructions by maintaining the property carefully.
✓ Use natural barriers and landscaping to limit access.
✓ Use fencing and other constructed barriers where appropriate.
✓ Use lighting that conforms to national lighting standards.
✓ Be certain that no attractive nuisances or hazardous materials accumulate in the area.
✓ Assign responsibilities for periodic inspections.
✓ Remove seasonal and natural hazards such as snow, ice, and fallen trees.

Recommended Enhancements

✓✓ Provide electronic intrusion detection equipment or recorded CCTV if warranted.
✓✓ Contract with off-duty police or security officers to prevent unauthorized use of open space.
✓✓ Use electronic access systems.

3.2.23 Outdoor Areas for Employees

Planning Considerations

- Separate outdoor areas for employees to control general public access.
- Use barriers to separate the areas from the general circulation pattern. The barriers could include landscaping, pools, planters, walls, or fencing.
- If outdoor areas provide direct access to the facility, they require the same standards of access control and protection as the facility's primary entrances.

- Recreation areas should have lighting and visibility consistent with hours of use.

Suggested Minimum Security Requirements

✓ Use appropriate signs to identify your organization's property boundaries, guide circulation and traffic patterns, post use-restriction notices, and provide appropriate warnings for the site.
✓ Use lighting that conforms to national standards.
✓ Provide ID badges for employees.
✓ Use smart locking systems with key control audit trail.

Recommended Enhancements

✓✓ Control access and prevent unauthorized use by following the guidelines set forth in your organization's access control and ID policy.
✓✓ Use recorded CCTV to monitor access activity.

3.2.24 Parking Lots, Ramps, Garages, and Buildings

Planning Considerations

- Data collected at the national level—the number of incidents, the types of incidents, and the resulting lawsuits—have helped to define what appropriate security means for this area.
- If possible, locate employee and nonemployee parking in an area physically separated from warehousing, shipping and receiving, manufacturing visitor parking, and non-company-related traffic and pedestrian flow.
- Separate traffic patterns as much as possible for deliveries, visitors, pedestrian, public, and trucking.
- Consider overflow or special events and the security of vehicles and persons during events.
- Plan for emergency services access and response.
- Plan for violation enforcement and disabled-vehicle removal.
- There must be access and security for the handicapped, in accordance with the Americans with Disabilities Act (ADA).
- Consider instituting additional site access restrictions or controls after normal or peak business hours.
- Identify all parking areas clearly and post appropriate signs.

- A different set of review and control procedures should be provided for underground and enclosed parking structures.
- Any entrances from underground, ramps, or controlled parking structures with direct access to the building require the same standards of access control and protection as the facility's primary entrances.

Suggested Minimum Security Requirements

✓ Use lighting that conforms to national lighting standards.
✓ Use appropriate signs to identify your organization's property boundaries, guide circulation and traffic patterns, post restriction notices, and provide appropriate warnings for the area.
✓ Limit the number of entry and exit points. Control the access at each point.
✓ Use barriers, both natural and constructed.

Recommended Enhancements

✓✓ Provide uniformed officers to escort personnel and to patrol the area.
✓✓ Use authorization labels or stickers for the vehicles allowed in the area.
✓✓ Use an electronic access control system.
✓✓ Use recorded CCTV with monitors. Post clear notifications to employees that specify the system you are using is for monitoring or response, but only if security staff resources are in place and trained to provide a response. Otherwise, avoid such a posting and the associated legal liabilities.

3.2.25 Public Restrooms

Planning Considerations

- Based on the visitor traffic volume and visitor need, consider whether this amenity is required at your location.
- Plan to locate restrooms in a public space that is exterior to areas which require escorts for visitors and visitor credentials.
- For facilities with low volume, plan for a single, unisex restroom.

Suggested Minimum Security Requirements

✓ Locate the restrooms so that they are available only to authorized personnel and registered visitors.

✓ Post the appropriate signs.

✓ For areas that are not isolated, control access by visual recognition.

Recommended Enhancements

✓✓ Provide locking hardware and devices on entry doors to restrooms or to stalls.

3.2.26 Public Safety and Emergency Response

Planning Considerations

- In planning for public safety and emergency response, it is absolutely critical that you integrate security into your business operations.
- Be certain that you gather input from every aspect of your business operations regarding the types of emergencies that could occur and the types of responses required.
- Equipment, space, and facilities planning must be completed for each potential emergency.
- Identify personnel, functions, and agencies that will be necessary for effective response to each emergency.
- Security hardware and security systems may be very effective in assisting with emergency responses when they are designed and used properly. Systems such as CCTV, radios, alarms, uniformed officers, liaisons to fire departments and law enforcement, and programs for emergency services may mean the difference between a successful response to an emergency and a disaster.
- Review related materials and communicate with the internal and external resources that have responsibilities relating to public safety and emergency response:
  - Safety
  - Industrial hygiene
  - Medical
  - IT
  - Public relations
  - Engineering
  - Federal, state, and local agencies

Suggested Minimum Security Requirements

✓ A local business emergency response plan must be developed that addresses all potential emergencies that have been identified.

✓ Develop a training and coordination plan.
✓ Conduct simulations of incidents and responses.
✓ Post signs that clearly mark internal and external access/egress routes.
✓ Periodically test emergency equipment. Replace all items that do not meet their performance standards.

Recommended Enhancements

✓✓ Coordinate simulations with community agencies.
✓✓ Film the exercises and review them for ways to improve.

3.2.27 Raw Materials Areas

Planning Considerations

- Locate raw materials in an area that is convenient for production and process flow, and for which you can provide security that is consistent with the risks to the material.
- Evaluate security risks on the potential and probability of misuse, as well as the value of the material.
- Provide a system of accountability that keeps the purchased amounts in balance with the inventory amount, the production rates, and the ratio of waste.

Suggested Minimum Security Requirements

✓ Control access to the materials area and prevent unauthorized use of materials.
✓ Use smart locking systems with key control.
✓ Provide fences, gates, barriers, and containers for the area.
✓ Post the appropriate signs.
✓ Use lighting that meets national standards.

Recommended Enhancements

✓✓ Use electronic access systems.
✓✓ Use recorded CCTV for monitoring activity.
✓✓ Use an automated production, material movement, and inventory control system linked to individuals and ID badges for an audit trail of material movements.

3.2.28 Reception Areas

Planning Considerations

- Reception areas must be designed to accommodate visitors, with every possible courtesy, until proper credentials and verification are complete.
- Position receptionists and security personnel so that they have maximum observation and control over their area. Position the receptionists and security personnel so they can greet, identify, sign-in, and coordinate the escorts for visitors, contractors, and vendors.
- Separate the reception area from the facility proper with a physical barrier.
- Receptionists must be able to deny access to those who are not authorized.
- Receptionists and security personnel also provide general visitor information. In addition, they often have phone and mail duties. Design their workstations so that these duties don't interfere with their security-related responsibilities.
- Provide basic amenities such as restrooms, telephone, and meeting rooms in the lobby for visitor, host, and employee use.
- Limit entrance to the remainder of the facility to a single point.

Suggested Minimum Security Requirements

- ✓ Each entry point must have access control that is in accordance with your organization's access control and ID policy.
- ✓ The decision whether to automate access control or to use a receptionist or security officer should be made in conjunction with your organization's security representative.
- ✓ Provide receptionists at building or perimeter points of entry with a distress alarm system that signals the need for assistance. In some situations, a silent alarm device that the receptionist can use to summon law enforcement personnel may be in order.
- ✓ Provide entry way and internal lighting that is adequate, especially during nights and the winter season. Follow national lighting standards.
- ✓ Nonresident organization employees, nonemployees, visitors, vendors, suppliers, and contractors should follow your organization's

access control and ID policy by wearing the appropriate credentials.

✓ Post appropriate signs to identify your organization's property boundaries, guide circulation and traffic patterns, post restriction notices, and provide appropriate warnings for the area.

✓ Plan for provision of remote control of external entrance door locks from the receptionist's work area.

✓ Link the receptionist's emergency duress button to the access control and alarm systems.

✓ Plan for and design appropriate training for the primary receptionist and the person(s) who provide temporary replacement, to ensure consistency.

Recommended Enhancements

✓✓ Provide remote door locking and unlocking controls for the exterior door and for the door between the receptionist and the rest of the facility.

✓✓ Provide receptionists with an evacuation door for their area; a secure copy room adjacent to the receptionist's work station provides a safe room option.

✓✓ Provide a 24-hour video camera and time/day/date recorder coverage that is activated by motion detection or alarm monitoring devices.

3.2.29 Research and Development Areas

Planning Considerations

• Plan to isolate research and development areas from public areas and from general circulation paths. See *Adjacency Factors* in Chapter 2 for more information.

• Provide appropriate furniture and storage units to secure restricted information, such as manuals and documents.

• Design this area with perimeter walls that reach all the way from the floor to the floor above.

• Provide audit trail capability for all projects.

• Plan for entrances and exits to the area that can be controlled to allow access to only the designated personnel.

Suggested Minimum Security Requirements

✓ Restrict access to authorized personnel.

✓ Provide access logs.
✓ Secure furniture and storage units.
✓ Use smart locking hardware with key control and audit trail.
✓ Escort all visitors and consulting personnel.
✓ Use an ID or badge system that is in accordance with your organization's policy.

Recommended Enhancements

✓✓ Use a card or PIN access system.
✓✓ Use recorded CCTV system with time/day/date recording software.
✓✓ Install intrusion detection devices with local alarms.
✓✓ Post the appropriate signs.
✓✓ Provide a receptionist for the area.

3.2.30 Roof Access

Planning Considerations

• Secure all skylights, air ducts, vents, elevator windows and other openings in the roof to prevent intrusion and/or visual or auditory observation of proprietary information or processes.
• Doors leading to the roof from inside the building should meet industrial grade construction standards and provide a level of security equal to that provided by the facility's perimeter entry points.
• Secure exterior ladders that lead to the roof to the level required to prevent unauthorized use.

Suggested Minimum Security Requirements

✓ Provide procedural controls that allow only authorized personnel to use the roof at authorized times.
✓ Be certain that your access system complies with your safety department's roof access procedures.
✓ Provide the appropriate signs.
✓ Use locking systems with key control that are consistent with the building perimeter standards.
✓ Provide an audit trail that is consistent with your building's security standards.

Recommended Enhancements

✓✓ Use recorded CCTV to monitor activity.

✓✓ Use an electronic access control system (card or PIN system) with an audit trail.
✓✓ Where exterior access is possible, use intrusion detection devices that are consistent with your building's security standards.

3.2.31 Sales and Marketing

Planning Considerations

- The risks to sales and marketing information, equipment, and facilities vary widely. The risks depend, to a large extent, on the geographic location and the business market.
- Complete risk assessments for each individual business unit in conjunction with your organization's security representative.
- Due to the requirements of public access and the business location requirements of most sales and marketing facilities, the amount and type of security is often underestimated.
- Business conditions, leased and maintenance facilities, extended working hours, public parking facilities, minimal staffing, increased information dissemination, and competitive conditions can all contribute to the need for enhanced security measures.

Suggested Minimum Security Requirements

✓ Use an access control system in accordance with your organization's policy.
✓ Control access, with an audit trail, to all areas during non-business hours.
✓ Control access to files, both electronic and physical.
✓ Provide secure containers and cabinets for storing information.
✓ Control electronic access in accordance with the standards provided by your organization's policies and IT procedures.
✓ Use a smart locking system with key control and audit trail.
✓ Use IT security procedures for marking, storing, and disseminating internal use and restricted information. Review these procedures on a regular basis.
✓ If you are in a multi-tenant facility, review the physical security guidelines on a regular basis.
✓ Provide for appropriate disposal of registered information.

Recommended Enhancements

✓✓ Install intrusion detection devices.
✓✓ Use an electronic access control system at the facility.
✓✓ Maintain a 24-7, camera-recording audit trail of designated entry and exit points.

3.2.32 Scrap and Salvage

Planning Considerations

- All local policies and procedures should be developed after an extensive review with your organization's security and resource recovery plans.
- Your organization's control over scrap or salvage material continues to the point when the material is sold, disposed of in a landfill, or destroyed. Periodically verify that this control is maintained.
- Alter the material that is to be disposed of to stop it from reentering the market or from being used in a way that is not intended by your organization.
- Due to the wide range of types and quantities of scrap and salvage material, risk assessment and physical security planning should take place in conjunction with your organization's security representative.

Suggested Minimum Security Requirements

✓ Control access to materials.
✓ Provide an audit trail of all access to and movement of material.
✓ Store material in a manner that reduces hazards and security risks and which allows for effective control until disposal.
✓ Disposal operations are governed by current and valid contracts. Compliance should be validated through periodic reviews and inspections.

Recommended Enhancements

✓✓ Some materials or operations may require visual observations and monitoring.
✓✓ During disposal, contact your organization's security representative to review risks and security measures.

3.2.33 Shipping and Receiving Areas

Planning Considerations

- To minimize the need for nonemployees, drivers, delivery people, and visitors to go beyond the shipping and receiving areas, provide a reception area equipped with a public restroom, telephone, and vending machines.
- Control access and exits at all dock and pedestrian doors leading into shipping and receiving areas and to dock floors.
- Maintain the same level of access control at shipping and receiving areas as at visitor and administrative entrances and exits.

Suggested Minimum Security Requirements

✓ Use appropriate door hardware on all doors.
✓ Control vehicle movements.
✓ Implement a reliable ID and/or badge system. This might be a card or PIN access system.
✓ Sign the area appropriately for movement procedures.
✓ Escort visitors and nonemployees when they leave the reception area. Designate an employee to serve as the escort.

Recommended Enhancements

✓✓ Control doors remotely from the work station of a security officer, receptionist, or designated employee.
✓✓ Keep a video audit trail of the interior areas.
✓✓ Use a recorded CCTV audit trail with time/day/date during scheduled business hours, and have the system activated by motion detection or alarm monitoring devices during nonbusiness hours.

3.2.34 Supply Rooms

Planning Considerations

- Assess the security level needed, based on the risk, volume, and consequences of lost or stolen supplies.
- Enclose supplies in dedicated secure rooms or cabinets.

Suggested Minimum Security Requirements

✓ Limit access to authorized personnel.
✓ Provide smart locking systems, with key control.

✓ Maintain an audit trail of access to supply rooms during non-business hours.
✓ Enclose supply rooms by walls that reach from the floor to the ceiling.
✓ Control access to supply rooms during non-business hours.
✓ Lock cabinets and containers during non-business hours.

Recommended Enhancements

✓✓ Use intrusion detection devices and maintain an audit trail of all activity.
✓✓ Use ID, badge, card, or PIN access systems that supplement your access control procedures.

3.2.35 Tool Rooms

Planning Considerations

• Keep tools in a central location that serves everyone who requires access to the tools. Have a single entrance and exit point from the location.
• Plan for a system that meets the business needs and provides accountability.
• Design the area with walls that reach from the floor to the floor above.

Suggested Minimum Security Requirements

• Limit access to the interior of the room to those personnel who have a business need to be there.
• Have an attendant monitor the room and maintain inventory of the tools.
• Secure the room if there is no attendant.
• Use smart locks and locking hardware with key control and audit trail to secure the room during non-business hours.

Recommended Enhancements

✓✓ Use a card access or PIN access system.
✓✓ Use recorded CCTV to monitor activity.
✓✓ Establish an inventory control system that uses an automated method of tool accountability.

3.2.36 Utility Equipment and Utility Rooms

Planning Considerations

- Utility equipment and utility rooms dedicated to equipment for security, telephones, computers, heating and air conditioning, gas, electricity, water, fuel, and fire require planning around considerations such as:
  - Criticality to the business;
  - Personnel requiring access to the area;
  - Location options available in the facility;
  - Hours of operations; and
  - Concurrent security measures.

Suggested Minimum Security Requirements

- ✓ Control access to the area.
- ✓ Use secure doors, with smart locking systems and key control.
- ✓ Post the appropriate signs.
- ✓ Provide an audit trail of all access activity.
- ✓ Use lighting in accordance with national standards.

Recommended Enhancements

- ✓✓ Use an alarm system with local response when the utilities, equipment, or processes are critical to your operations.
- ✓✓ Provide fencing for the area.
- ✓✓ Use a recorded CCTV audit trail.
- ✓✓ Use electronic card access with an audit trail.

3.2.37 Warehouses, Mail Rooms, and Shipping/Receiving

Planning Considerations

- Design truck dock areas to control access and limit nonemployee movements to the dock space and dock operations. Nonemployees access should be in accordance with your organization's policy, including escort requirements.
- Maintain the same level of access control at shipping and receiving areas as at visitor and administrative entrances and exits.
- The dock office should be located adjacent to the dock area. It should be equipped with windows for providing clear observation of operations.

- Plan for the capability to authorize entry from a remote location, such as a security office, a receptionist's desk, or a designated employee's work station.
- To minimize the need for nonemployees, drivers, delivery people, and visitors to go beyond the mail and the shipping and receiving areas, provide a delivery or a reception area equipped with a public restroom, telephone, drinking water, and vending machines.
- Plan for ventilation point controls that will not compromise security.
- Control access and exits at dock and pedestrian doors leading into shipping and receiving areas and to dock floors.
- Plan for adequate vehicle access control, vehicle movement, and employee parking that does not compromise site security.

Suggested Minimum Security Requirements

- ✓ Use ID and nonemployee credentials in accordance with your organization's access control and ID policy.
- ✓ Use carrier and driver claim history analysis to choose and monitor reliable carriers and drivers.
- ✓ Analyze customer complaints to see if there is a pattern of vandalism, sabotage, theft, or contamination.
- ✓ Analyze your claims history to look for patterns of loss.
- ✓ Minimize the number of access points.
- ✓ Use hardware that is consistent with hardware used throughout the rest of the building.
- ✓ Separate the employee parking area from the warehouse parking area.
- ✓ Control vehicle movements. Limit door openings to authorized vehicles.
- ✓ Store returned goods, opened cases, and claims materials in a secured, access-controlled area.
- ✓ Access to the dock areas from the waiting areas must be controlled.
- ✓ Install fences with secure gates.
- ✓ Post the appropriate signs, and provide a doorbell for entry requests.
- ✓ Provide an audit trail and individual PINs on metered postage machines.
- ✓ Provide procedural controls to monitor personal, unauthorized, or questionable use of these areas, including mail, postage, and shipping.

Recommended Enhancements

✓✓ Secure exterior doors with alarm devices.

✓✓ Use an electronic access system to control access to shipping and receiving doors, docks, warehouses, mail rooms, and shipping and receiving areas.

✓✓ Use a recorded CCTV audit trail with time/day/date during scheduled business hours, and have the system activated by motion detection or alarm monitoring devices during non-business hours.

3.2.38 Windows

Planning Considerations

- Windows should provide light and ventilation but not allow easy access, either visual or physical, into a facility.
- Windows should be unobstructed from view.
- If they can be opened, secure the windows to a level equal to the requirements of the contents of the space.

Suggested Minimum Security Requirements

✓ Use appropriate locking hardware.

Recommended Enhancements

✓✓ Use shatter-resistant film.

✓✓ Install microwave or passive infrared motion detectors near the windows.

✓✓ Use sensors that detect shock or glass breakage.

3.2.39 Zone 4

Planning Considerations

- There are special areas of your business that may require security beyond that which is normally provided for most areas of your business. Most areas require a Zone 1, 2, or 3 level of protection; however, these special areas need a Zone 4 protection level (see Chapter 2 for more information on the zones of security).
- It is more cost effective to provide enhanced security for small areas of your business than to bring the level of security for the entire business up to the level required by the area of highest risk.

- The list below includes many of the areas considered to be Zone 4 or restricted areas. The list does not include all possibilities; it is meant to help to assess your business in terms of the areas that may need Zone 4 protection.
  - Research and development
  - Laboratories
  - Proprietary production or process areas
  - High-value parts or sensitive parts storage areas
  - Data storage
  - Tool rooms and cribs
  - Personnel and records areas
  - Cash handling and storage areas
  - New products and pilot plant areas
  - Access control and security systems
  - Hazardous materials storage
  - Functions and operations that are critical to the business (for example, incinerators, one-of-a-kind machinery, utility area, materials area)
  - Executive or other employee at risk
- Each Zone 4 area must be evaluated separately for the security level required. Identify the level of risk and the consequences of loss by gathering information from the other areas that rely on the area under evaluation.
- Isolate your Zone 4 areas from normal traffic flow. Locate these areas in operationally effective places without compromising security through unnecessary access, observation, or use.
- Limit the number of entrances and exits from the area.
- Plan for operational contingencies to handle the occurrence of the most likely emergency situations. These emergencies might be natural or caused by people.
- Plan to use construction techniques, equipment, furniture, and security systems that provide the level of protection required by the risk to and criticality of the operation.
- Plan for emergency backup to utility services. Plan to have an alternative source of energy and backup capabilities consistent with the security and operational needs of the business.
- Plan for system backups in: equipment, parts, data, documents, services, facilities, and people. Cross-training is the best way to back up the people skills required for effective security.

Suggested Minimum Security Requirements

✓ Post signs that define the restricted area and the appropriate procedures for the area.

✓ Control access to the area; only authorized people, at authorized times, may access the area. Provide an audit trail of all access activity.

✓ Use smart locking hardware, with key control and audit trail, on all the appropriate furniture, storage cabinets, files, and equipment.

✓ Screen nonassigned personnel and brief them before they use the area. Depending on the circumstances, this may include background checks, signed nondisclosure agreements, parcel and vehicle inspections, and safety briefings.

✓ Develop and use company escort procedures or employ a more restrictive set of escort procedures if the situation warrants. You may need to institute procedures that require higher-level management authorization, two-person occupancy, or business-partner approval.

✓ Use an ID badge system in accordance with your organization's policies.

✓ Establish appropriate controls on waste and scrap.

✓ Brief the employees regularly on security-related issues.

✓ Review purchasing, shipping, and receiving procedures regularly to maintain the appropriate level of security.

✓ Keep cabinets and containers locked when not in use.

✓ Establish and maintain an inventory of critical items. Frequently verify the accuracy of your inventory counts.

Recommended Enhancements

✓✓ Use recorded CCTV, with day/time/date software, to monitor access activity and provide audit trail.

✓✓ Use electronic access control systems that are designed to monitor and control piggybacking.

✓✓ Use intrusion detection devices and maintain an audit trail of all activity.

✓✓ Many operations and situations require special construction, equipment, hardware, controls, and procedures to bring an area up to a Zone 4 level of protection. Contact your organization's security representative or an outside consultant for assistance with assessing how well your security measures are meeting your Zone 4 requirements.

CHAPTER 4

Performance Specifications

4.1 INTRODUCTION

This chapter provides performance specifications for the security measures that may be applied to the business areas, functions, and processes described in Chapter 3.

Figure 4.1 provides a quick overview of the organization of this chapter. The 38 main topics are arranged in alphabetic order. Many of the topics have subsections, which are also arranged alphabetically under their main topic.

4.2 ACCESS CONTROL

Access control requires that only designated entrances and exits are used for all authorized pedestrian and vehicle traffic, in both protected areas and the entire facility.

- An audit trail (a permanent record) of certain types of activities is required.
- Local management must determine the degree of control necessary to meet the specific operational and security needs of their business.

4.2.1 Piggybacking and Tailgating

Piggybacking and tailgating are two forms of unauthorized entry at an access control point.

- Piggybacking occurs when an unauthorized person follows an authorized person through an access control point. For example, Mr. Johnson, who is an organization employee, holds the door open for another person who does not have organization authorization for access.
- Tailgating occurs when an unauthorized person enters an organization's facility through an access control point as an authorized person leaves. For example, Ms. Smith, who is not authorized to enter

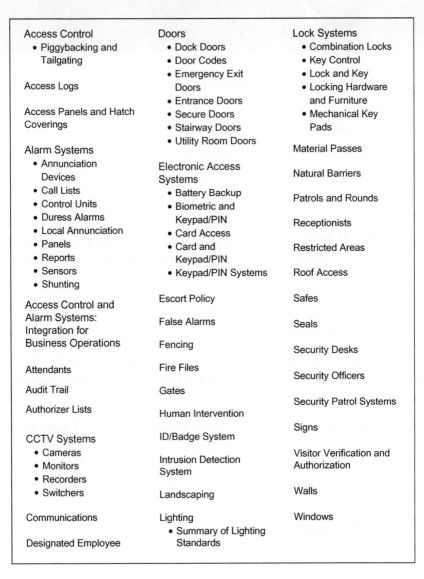

Figure 4.1 Chapter 4 Outline.

the facility, waits outside the delivery door until the delivery person leaves. She steps inside the facility before the door is closed.

It is the responsibility of authorized persons to control access when they open a door for their own use. Use educational programs to make people aware of their responsibility in this important area of access control.

4.3 ACCESS LOGS

Access logs are used to maintain a record of all the individuals entering and exiting an organization's facility: visitors during business hours, and all employees and visitors during non-business hours.

Access information is required by your organization for the express purpose of managing the safety and security of people during the time they are on your organization's property.

Access logs must be retained for at least two years. The minimum information required for an access log is

- Your organization's building number (if applicable);
- Individual's name;
- Point of entry or exit; and
- Time of entry and exit.

For visitors, additional information is required:

- The company the visitor represents
- Contact person (person being visited)
- Person authorizing the visit
- Person escorting the visitor
- Purpose of the visit
- Visitor's citizenship, if required by your organization's government contracts department

4.4 ACCESS PANELS AND HATCH COVERINGS

Access panels and hatch covers ensure that only authorized personnel gain access to utility equipment.

- For security and durability reasons, metal panels and covers are recommended.
- It's also recommended that the panels and covers use either lock and key or special fasteners, or that they be locked from inside a secured area.

4.5 ALARM SYSTEMS

An alarm system is an assembly of equipment designed and arranged to signal the presence of a situation that requires immediate attention.

For example, unauthorized entry or exit, fire, temperature rise, chemical spill, and monitor point shunting are all conditions that require immediate attention.

An alarm system may be local to the building proper, central to an on-site proprietary monitoring station, or connected to an off-site central monitoring station.

An alarm system must be 100 percent reliable:

* In detecting events that need immediate attention, and
* In not indicating an alarm condition when no alarm situation exists.

An alarm system can have many different components and configurations. The next nine subsections describe the major components of an alarm system.

4.5.1 Annunciation Devices

Annunciation is the sounding of audible tones or the display of visible signals. Annunciation devices provide auditory and/or visual alert of an alarm condition such as an intrusion, fire, or other hazardous situation.

* Annunciation devices include electronic bells, buzzers, horns, flashing lights, flags, lamps, and strobes.
* For auditory devices, be certain to specify an appropriate decibel level so that the device can be heard within its immediate physical environment.
* For visual devices, be certain that the lights are clearly visible above the ambient lighting.
* Develop appropriate response procedures for each alarm condition that may be signaled by the annunciation devices.
* Conduct periodic integrity tests to verify the performance of the annunciation devices and the alarm system.

4.5.2 Call Lists

A call list is a list of people, departments, and organizations to be called in case of an alarm condition. Your organization's procedures require that the time of each alarm is documented and that the appropriate people are notified each time an alarm occurs.

* The people, departments, and organizations in call lists are usually arranged in order of priority by alarm type. The first people to be

contacted in case of a specific alarm are listed first, with other people listed in descending order of priority.

- A call list should include the name, address, telephone number, emergency phone number, and contact person (if appropriate) for each person, department, and organization on the list.
- Create a written report to provide an audit trail for each alarm. The report documents the alarm date and time, the cause of the alarm, the name of the person from the call list who was contacted, as well as the date and time of the contact.

4.5.3 Control Units

An alarm control unit is an electronic device, usually a key pad, that provides a communication interface between the alarm system's panels and the human operator. The control unit may also produce an alarm signal when its programming indicates that an alarm condition exists.

- Provide back-up power for both the control unit and the alarm sensors.
- Locate the control unit near a designated 24-hour entry point so that authorized personnel can access the unit easily.
- Provide a programmable time delay so that the unit can be armed and disarmed from within the space protected by the system.
- Provide advance warning of the alarm system's arming status using audio and LED light annunciation.
- Control access to the system by limiting PINs to authorized personnel. See the *Keypad/PIN* section under *Electronic Access Systems* later in this chapter for more information.
- Define, document, and maintain the system's operating and reporting procedures.

4.5.4 Duress Alarms

A duress alarm is recommended for individuals and workstations that may be exposed to safety or security risks.

- A duress alarm requires a "hold up" button that is strategically placed out of the view of the public.
- The alarm's annunciation must be undetectable in the hold-up button's immediate area.
- Annunciation must be located in areas where human response is guaranteed.

- Annunciation should include audible tones combined with strobe lights. Duress alarms must be noticed immediately.

4.5.5 Local Annunciation

Alarms that are annunciated locally (i.e., at the source of the alarm) are used to deter unauthorized activity.

- It identifies the point of the unauthorized activity and calls attention to the area.
- It notifies the individual that he or she has caused an alarm and that a security-related response may be forthcoming, even if the alarm was unintentional or caused by human error.
- Alarm devices should be armed and protected from tampering. In cold climates, local battery-operated devices are not dependable and are not recommended
- Establish maintenance procedures for all alarms.
- Hard-wired systems that also transmit signals to a central location are preferred over those that just annunciate locally.
- Appropriate signs should accompany alarms to discourage individuals from creating an alarm condition. For example, "Emergency Exit Only. Alarm Will Sound," should be posted on alarm doors to deter unauthorized activity.

4.5.6 Panels

An alarm panel is an electronic panel secured within a metal cabinet. The panel is designed to receive and process the electronic signals sent from the various alarm monitors and sensors distributed throughout the protected area. The panel is the "brain" of the alarm system.

The alarm panel should be located in a secure room or a secure equipment closet.

- Access to the panel must be limited to authorized personnel. Access is typically gained through a key pad. See the *Keypad/PIN* section under *Electronic Access Systems* later in this chapter for more information.
- Lock the alarm panel.
- Monitor unauthorized access to the panel with an electromagnetic tamper switch.

Note: In some small systems, especially if there is only one entrance to a facility, the control unit and the panel are combined in one component.

4.5.7 Reports
Written reports provide permanent records and audit trails of alarm system activity.

- Alarm notification report: Every time an alarm occurs that results in a call to a person, department, or organization listed on an emergency or alarm call list, a report must be generated that shows:
  - The time of the alarm;
  - The time of the call;
  - Who was notified; and
  - The final determination of the cause of the alarm (for example, there was an actual burglary and the police were called, or there was an undetermined alarm from a faulty sensing device that now requires testing, repair, or replacement).
- Opening and closing exception report: This report lists all the times a facility opens earlier than or closes later than the time designated by management. The report must contain the following information:
  - The time the facility was opened or closed.
  - The person who opened or closed the facility.
- Authorized individuals report: This report shows all the individuals who are authorized to access the alarm system in order to arm (activate) or disarm (deactivate) it. This report must be reviewed by management on a regular basis (i.e., at least once per year) and updated whenever a change to the list of authorized people occurs.

All alarm system reports should be provided to your organization's management on a regular basis. The frequency of these reports should be determined by local organization management.

4.5.8 Sensors
Alarm sensors are devices that detect events that are not part of the normal working environment and that send signals to the alarm panel for processing.

- Alarm sensors, whether mechanical or electronic, must be strategically placed so that they can monitor conditions that require security alerts.

- Special care must be taken when designing alarm sensor systems so that they resist and prevent tampering and protect equipment from damage.
- Secure control boxes, external bells, and junction boxes for all alarm systems with high quality locks, or provide some type of alert if the alarm device has been tampered with or opened.
- Provide protective covering for surface-mounted contact switches, wire connections, and wire distributions. These protective coverings must be strong enough to withstand damage due to collisions and bumps.
- Alarm sensors need a power supply that cannot be interrupted. Backups and/or batteries are usually required.
- Whenever possible, recess door contact monitor switches.
- Connect the alarm system with the CCTV system where appropriate.

There are four common types of alarm sensors:

1. Magnetic contact switches
2. Motion detection devices, both single element and dual element sensors
3. Glass break protection devices
4. Photoelectric and microwave beam devices

4.5.8.1 Magnetic Contact Switches

Magnetic contact switches consist of two separate units that are attached to a hinged or sliding door or window. One unit, the magnet, is attached to the door or window. The other unit is an actuated switch that is mounted on the frame. When the door or window is opened, the magnetic contact is broken, and the alarm sensor is activated.

- Additional protection can be obtained using balanced switches. Regular magnetic contact switches can be tampered with through the use of an external magnet. Balanced switches, however, operate by creating a balanced magnetic field that detects increases or decreases in the sensor's magnetic field strength.
- Balanced switches are recommended in any application that calls for magnetic contact switches.
- Recessing switches are also recommended to reduce potential tampering with the device and the connecting wires.

4.5.8.2 Motion Detection Devices

Motion detection devices are part of most alarm systems. There are many different types of motion detectors and a variety of sensor technologies: ultrasonic waves, infrared light waves, microwave (electromagnetic) fields, and passive infrared (heat sensors).

Single element detectors use just one type of technology (for example, ultrasonic waves); dual element detectors combine technologies (for example, ultrasonic waves and heat sensors) to provide better detection.

Single element detectors are limited in their capabilities:

- Single element sensor technologies each may have limitations that cause them to emit their own type of false alarm. For example, heating and air conditioning air flow, heat build-up from the sun or appliances, outside vibrations from traffic or wind, machinery movement, printers, faxes, and the intrusions of small animals or insects can fool single element technologies, causing the sensor to inappropriately signal a detected motion.
- The use of dual element sensors will reduce the false alarms caused by the limitations of the single element sensor.

Dual element sensors incorporate two separate technologies into a single sensor to reduce the false alarms caused by the limitations of each type of motion sensor:

- Dual element sensors analyze the signals from two different types of sensors. For example, a heat detector (passive infrared) and a change in sound pattern detector (ultrasonic) might be combined.
- Alarm signals are sent only when the alarm threshold of both detectors is reached.
- Since detectors tend to be most susceptible to one type of "false" alarm, detectors can be combined into a dual element so that each type's limitations are offset by the other type's strengths.
- The sensors must be self-checking and resistant to tampering and sabotage.

4.5.8.3 Glass Break Protection Devices

Glass break devices are designed to detect the breakage of glass. They are not necessarily attached to a window; often they are mounted away from the glass area and aimed in a manner that allows each device to monitor a portion of the glass.

- Dual element glass break devices are recommended. The most common combination of sensor elements include one that monitors the shock wave set up by the breaking of glass and one that responds to the unique frequencies corresponding to the sound of breaking glass.
- Dual element eliminates the false alarms from the sudden noise and vibrations in glass areas caused by high winds.

4.5.8.4 Beam Sensors

The most common types of beam sensors are photoelectric and microwave. These beam systems are designed to control and project narrow beams, creating a protective linear sensing barrier. Photoelectric systems are highly reliable for interior applications, and microwave systems have been heavily focused on exterior applications.

The most economical beam sensor is photoelectric technology. Photoelectric is also used as a safety device for the protection from opened doors, docks, and shafts. Warehouse applications, where banks of overhead doors may be, can be economically covered with a single beam.

One issue for warehouse shipping and receiving doors is the design requirement to only open a dock door when a truck is actually in the dock bay. Photo beams work well in this application and signal systems for door closures when the truck departs. In addition, for automatic door closures, the photo beam works well to ensure that the door opening is no longer obstructed and will close automatically only when the zone is clear, similar to home garage electric door systems.

For exterior applications, microwave has been a formidable system to establish perimeters, but must have a direct line of sight and a terrain that is relatively level and free of trees and extreme grade changes. Multiple grade changes require additional transmitters and receivers, making this application uneconomical. In addition, fog, heavy rain, and snow will degrade or interrupt the microwave's transmission and signal. Government applications have been the primary users of this technology.

4.5.9 Shunting

Alarm shunt devices are used to deliberately turn off (or short out) a portion of an electrical circuit and the alarm sensors attached to that portion of the circuit. Shunting is required when the alarm system needs maintenance, or when a business need arises (such as use of a particular door that normally causes an alarm).

- Only authorized personnel are allowed access to a shunt device. Access to the device is usually controlled by a key pad with PIN control, or by a key-operated switch.
- An audit trail of all shunt device access is required.

4.6 ACCESS CONTROL AND ALARM SYSTEMS: INTEGRATION FOR BUSINESS OPERATIONS

The alarm systems and elements outlined above are traditional, closed, stand-alone alarm system models and designs that have been the common baseline approach for internal systems and external central alarm station alarm services for decades. Unfortunately, in today's work environments, most businesses no longer close at the end of the business day, lock-up, turn on their alarm systems, and go home. For many employees and businesses coming and going all day and night, the facilities never really close. Then how do you deal with alarms?

Most businesses address this as an integration issue of running and managing three systems—intrusion, fire, and access control—where access control has the ability to monitor and notify and is more flexible to tailoring the system to meet operational changes.

Fire systems must be stand-alone systems to meet the requirements of insurance underwriters as well as building codes. This system is best considered as a central station application.

Intrusion systems require a contiguous collection of sensors, armed in zones or point to point, with a breach of the system creating an alarm and generating a notification to management. For authorized individuals, strategically located keypads are distributed to arm and disarm the system and its zones. With today's flexible work schedules, the challenge to this traditional intrusion system is the number of people authorized to enter and disarm the system as well as the task to rearm when the last person is leaving the facility. Companies with more than 25–30 employees begin to face challenges with the proper arming and disarming of their intrusion systems.

Motion sensors for interior zones are also a problem today because of the dynamics of people circulation within the interior spaces. False alarms have become a frustrating and a costly reality as the alarm fines by your local city police will be levied after a pattern of as little as three alarms annually. Many companies have gone to private security when false alarm fines have become a problem. For many companies, the interior motion detectors have been replaced with the deployment of perimeter glass break sensors as a component of a perimeter protection system. Only the high-risk and low-traffic spaces still deploy motion sensors.

Many companies with electronic access control systems have moved to a hybrid approach where the use of dedicated card readers have been deployed to arm and disarm an intrusion system, eliminating the need to manage proprietary codes.

Another approach of companies with electronic access control is to designate authorized non-business hours doors for flexible work schedule entries and exits and manage these doors and alarms through their access control system. The glass break sensors and fire-exit only and non-business-hour doors and access points remain locked down and monitored through the intrusion alarm system.

Finally, many companies with electronic access control systems, and the majority of their employees with smart phones, have taken a critical look at their intrusion system's monthly monitoring fees and have elected to reduce their costs and move their entire intrusion monitoring over to their access control systems. They now receive all alarms through their access control system and pass their alarms to a security command center (SOC) and/or receive their alarm notifications through their smart phones.

4.7 ATTENDANTS

Attendants may be security officers, receptionists, employees, or contractors assigned to a specific location. Attendants are used to control access and to provide informational assistance to your organization's employees and visitors.

Locate the attendants strategically within the space to optimize their ability to control access and provide service.

For more information, see the *Human Intervention*, *Receptionists*, and *Security Officers* sections later in this chapter.

4.8 AUDIT TRAIL

An audit trail is a document or record of individuals entering and exiting your organization's facilities. Your access control and ID policy should require that an audit trail be maintained at all your organization's facilities.

Audit trails typically include written records or the electronic reading and recording of an individual's access key, access code, or ID badge. It's recommended that the date and time recordings of the individual's entry and exit activities are also included in the audit trail.

In addition to audit trails, access logs are often used to procedurally satisfy the policy.

4.9 AUTHORIZER LISTS

An authorizer is an organization employee who can authorize access for a nonemployee. Authorizer lists are maintained for each of your organization's facilities and areas.

The lists are used during the visitor verification process to ensure that all visitors, vendors, suppliers, and visiting employees are cleared for entrance to an area, a technology, or a process by a resident manager, supervisor, or designated employee who has responsibility for the specific area, technology, or process to which the visitor is seeking access.

Your organization's authorizer lists must be reviewed and updated at least once each year. Each list must contain the following information:

- Name of your organization's authorizer
- Authorizer's employee number
- Authorizer's telephone number
- Authorizer's organization address
- Department name and number

Your organization's authorizer lists are a key component in visitor access control. These lists should be kept as short as possible to maintain appropriate levels of security. See *Visitor Verification and Authorization* later in this chapter for more information on controlling visitor access.

4.10 CCTV SYSTEMS

Closed-circuit television (CCTV) provides video observation of remote locations. A CCTV system has four basic components:

- Cameras
- Monitors
- Recorders
- Switchers

CCTV is only one component in a total security system. It is an excellent tool for general surveillance, assessment, and verification, but it should never be considered the core of your security system or as a first response system. CCTV serves as an excellent backup to other security components, but it is not a stand-alone system. With today's systems evolving to digital technology, many camera systems have upgraded to digital, IP addressed cameras, now installed on the IT networks of the company's backbone and data switch.

CCTV can raise false expectations among employees, visitors, and vendors. Many people expect that CCTV means that security will respond immediately to their needs. The display of cameras can have a deterrent effect for general security issues, but will not deter serious security threats. If you use CCTV, you should periodically remind employees, visitors, and vendors about the level of protection provided by the system. The success of your security system depends on the degree to which all its components are integrated into an effective whole. Do not overestimate the value of CCTV technology as a cure-all for your security needs.

4.10.1 Cameras

Cameras are the remote eyes of your security system. They are an excellent tool for monitoring your operations.

- For optimum image quality and minimum maintenance costs, use solid digital, IP, and state chip (CCD) cameras.

- For interior and daytime exterior applications, color cameras are preferable to black and white. However, for nighttime applications, older, non-digital color cameras require higher levels of lighting. Due to the continuing reduction of camera costs, some sites have found it most effective to combine digital color and black and white cameras in a single installation for exterior applications.
- Using lights, light bars, and other auxiliary infrared lighting in conjunction with a CCTV system can dramatically increase the system's effectiveness.
- Using pan, tilt, and zoom (PTZ) equipment on the cameras can add flexibility to secondary cameras, but also creates dead zones of non-continuous coverage. We recommend using PTZ cameras only for general surveillance; fixed position cameras are preferable for most applications. The newer digital cameras now offer the wider angle of a fixed camera, where the software allows a variety of playback views selected by the operator, yet a complete digital image of the entire field is available. This technology has dramatically reduced the cost of the traditional PTZ camera.
- Use color cameras and color monitors to achieve maximum identification and verification.

4.10.2 Monitors

Monitors are used to display and view camera images.

The minimum screen size recommended for a single person viewing a monitor is nine inches; for alarm verification and simultaneous viewing, monitor screen size should be 12 to 15 inches. When multiple camera images are displayed on a single monitor, use a monitor that is at least 15 inches. Color monitors are recommended for all color cameras. Using your old monochrome monitors with your new color cameras limits the identification and verification effectiveness of a color camera.

Since it is difficult for humans to effectively watch a monitor continuously for more than about 30 minutes, we recommend using motion detection to send alarm signals to the work station where the monitoring is taking place. This helps to increase the security officer's effectiveness by reducing the need for continuous monitoring and by providing alerts to events that need to be attended to in real time. Digital systems also provide digital replay of images recorded prior to the programmed alarm. The prerecorded, prealarm recording is defined within the software.

4.10.3 Recorders

Time-lapse video recorders help augment the effectiveness of security monitoring. In fact, use of a CCTV system is not recommended if recorders are not part of the system. Digital technology now offers full recording through the network and software with digital playback. Recording capacities and retention are dependent upon the size of your network's server(s).

- Use commercial-grade recorders for your older applications and plan for systems upgrades to digital technology as budgets permit.
- Video recording provides an audit trail of activity. It helps your system meet the high standards required by modern security.
- Video recording also helps to provide answers to questions of time and identity when a security incident occurs. Use only recorders and/or software that include day/date/time in the visual record.
- Keep visual recordings of activity on file for at least 30 days.
- Recording by itself cannot help with real time assessment of an alarm condition. Use alarm sensor signals sent through the video signal channel and software to alert the assigned security officer or attendant that a real time alarm or event requires a response.
- Develop and keep current a set of written procedures for maintaining your recorders and/or recording software setup parameters.
- Video recording provides a backup in a layered system. Be certain that your access control procedures are integrated with the audit trail provided by your video recording.
- The minimum specifications for your recording include: day/date/ time display, input and output channels for responding to alarm sensors, programmable speeds for time-lapse recording, and a minimum recording capability of 720 hours.

4.10.4 Switchers

Video switchers are an option for multiple camera systems and are best suited for general surveillance only. A video switcher switches between cameras, giving you a set of video snapshots from the cameras connected to the switcher. Video switchers are now obsolete and replaced by the continuous recording capabilities of digital technology and networked systems. Consult your security coordinator and IT for their professional input on the merits of a systems upgrade to digital.

- With switchers, you are limited in coverage because the camera scene covered at any particular moment may not be the one you want covered. Switchers create dead zones in your video-monitoring coverage.
- Video motion detection is also not an option when switchers are employed. Digital technologies offer video motion detection as a software feature.

The term switch is now associated with the rack-mounted data switch blades inside IT data and server rooms. With the advancements of digital technology, both video cameras and select access control components are now digital, with IP addresses for network installations. Security systems now reside inside IT secure room environments. Now that security has space within IT spaces and the systems are digitally supported by IT, security is merely a resident on the IT network, plugged into available ports on IT's data switch.

Even though IT speaks in terms of 24-7 service for their network and devices, they too must perform maintenance. Unfortunately, IT 24-7 does not mean all devices on their system. When maintenance is to be scheduled, ensure that IT knows to coordinate with your security coordinator. It's strongly recommended that all patch cables connected to the IT switch are a special color, for example, red. That way, when IT is performing maintenance, it can be easily communicated that no red cables are to be disconnected or ports unpowered. A work-around maintenance scheme must be applied to maintain security's true 24-7 requirements for both electronic access control and video surveillance/audit trail.

4.11 COMMUNICATIONS

Clear and timely communication is central to the role of today's security officer. Effective responses to emergencies (life-threatening situations, natural disasters, and chemical spills) and security threats (theft, sabotage, and loss of sensitive information) depend upon the accurate and swift relay of information. Advances in technology and increased mobility continue to emphasize the fact that the modern security officer must be well versed in the use of all new communication systems:

- Computer networks
- Intercoms

- Paging systems
- Radio communications
- Telephone systems

Communication and security systems need to be integrated for optimizing security performance, maximizing resources, and enhancing service delivery. A communication system that is well integrated into the functions of your safety, industrial hygiene, fire protection, medical, management, and media departments enhances security's ability to respond to emergencies, control access, share information, and provide notification and verification. Cellular technologies, along with digital data transmission and fiber optic networks, provide alarm monitoring, intercom, paging, and mobile patrol capabilities that were not previously available.

4.12 DESIGNATED EMPLOYEE

A designated employee is an organization employee who has been assigned security responsibilities such as the following:

- Key control
- Materials control
- Access control
- Surveillance
- Verification
- Systems validation/testing

4.13 DOORS

All doors must meet building code requirements for the building's particular use and occupancy.

Doors should be of commercial or industrial grade materials and construction. All perimeter and interior secure doors must be equipped with the appropriate locking device and opening and closing hardware to resist forced entry or tampering from the outside. For access-controlled doors, electrified locking hardware with the option of built-in micro-switched request-to-exit (REX) signals back to the access system is recommended for maximum signal performance and systems reliability. The use of this locking hardware type dramatically reduces the possibility of false door forced alarms. For details on electrified locking hardware, consult with your security coordinator or an outside consultant.

Secure doors must also be equipped with a detection device and monitored to ensure that they return to a closed and locked position after being opened.

4.13.1 Dock Doors

Traditionally, access control is weak in areas that contain dock doors (e.g., shipping and receiving, warehouses). Sound operational procedures and management support are required to maintain access security in dock door areas.

- Dock doors must lock from the inside and be inaccessible from the outside.
- Use dock levelers that cannot be lowered below the dock/floor level when the dock door is in a down position; this prevents the creation of a crawl space.
- The doorway for the dock should include a security grate or screen if the door remains open for ventilation.
- Use a standard configuration for dock doors that includes sensors which determine whether a vehicle is present. The sensors prevent the door from opening when no vehicle is present.
- The dock should have dock locks that hold the truck in place while the door is open.

4.13.2 Door Codes

All doors at a site should be numbered and coded with a tag or a decal for identification.

- A door code numbering system enables employees, security officers, and maintenance personnel to identify a specific door quickly.
- Maintain a database containing these door numbering codes. Be certain to integrate locking and operating information on all doors that have locking and/or special operating hardware into the database.

4.13.3 Emergency Exit Doors

Emergency exit doors must be secure and work without fail in an emergency situation.

- At a minimum, install interior wire seals on emergency exit doors (and monitor for indications of unauthorized use) and place signs that indicate that the doors are to be used only in an emergency.
- Equip emergency exit doors with an alarm that is audible at the door and is annunciated at the security monitoring station when the door is opened.
- Any hinge pins on the exterior of the door must be secured.
- The outside of the door should not have any knobs, pulls, handles, or key cylinders.
- Emergency doors must be operable without any special knowledge. Use crash bars or simple door knobs.
- Equip the doors with hardware designed to ensure that the doors open, close, and are resecured without fail.

4.13.4 Entrance Doors

Entrance doors are used to control access to the authorized points of entry for employees, visitors, and vendors. Entrance doors, if staffed by a security officer, receptionist, or attendant, may be left unlocked during business hours.

- Limit the number of doors used for normal entrances and exits.
- All entrance doors must be capable of being closed, secured, and monitored.
- For staffed entrances where intrusions can occur, we recommend that a remote, electronically controlled, door-locking device be installed at a receptionist or security station near the entrance.

4.13.5 Secure Doors

Secure doors are those that control access to a building or an area.

- All doors leading to the outside (i.e., perimeter doors) are, by definition, secure doors.
- Secure doors must be monitored to ensure that they are in a closed and locked position.

4.13.6 Stairway Doors

Stairway doors can lead either to the outside, or be internal.

- If a stairway door exits directly to the outside, the door must be secure.
- Secure the stairway doors inside of multi-tenant buildings from the inside (the office side) with the appropriate locking hardware. The

outside of the door (the side in the stairwell) may have two options: 1. If access from the stairwell is unauthorized, the door should not have any operating knobs, handles, or key cylinders; 2. If vertical circulation between floors using the stairwell typically occurs, the entry onto the floor must be controlled with access by key or electronic access control. The electronic access control option is strongly recommended; consider this door to be a perimeter door to your facility's perimeter where an audit trail is also recommended.

• Any hinge pins on the exterior of the door must be secured.

4.13.7 Utility Room Doors

Utility room doors (e.g., doors to building equipment rooms, electrical closets, or telephone rooms) must be secure and access must be restricted.

• For rooms accessed by fewer than 30 people, use manual locks and keys. Smart keys are recommended for audit trail, as a hybrid lower-cost audit-trail solution. Keys need to be controlled by security or by management. See *Key Control* in the *Lock Systems* section later in this chapter for more information.

• For rooms accessed by more than 30 people, we recommend using electronic access control with audit trails.

4.14 ELECTRONIC ACCESS SYSTEMS

Electronic access systems, or card and PIN access systems, are used to control access into and out of an area. The card or PIN may be used alone or in combination to electronically control access.

There are a number of electronic access systems available. In general, there are four main types of electronic access systems:

1. Biometric and keypad/PIN access systems
2. Card or key fob access systems
3. Card or key fob and keypad/PIN access systems
4. Keypad/PIN access systems

4.14.1 Battery Backup

All electronic access systems must plan for situations that involve the loss of the primary power source. A battery backup must be designed into the overall system plan so that it is part of the total system's functionality.

The backup battery must power not only the processing system panels, but also the door locks, sensors, and all other peripheral equipment (for example, door contacts, motion detectors, touch bars, and push-button shunt devices). To avoid possible power spikes and data interruption of your access control system, do not combine the powering of your processor panes with your electronic locking hardware. It is strongly recommended that you isolate the power of your processing panels; never attempt to combine power supplies!

Be certain to carefully scrutinize the battery backups provided by many system manufacturers. They often fail to address the peripheral parts that play an integral part in the system functioning properly. Batteries are inexpensive; connect additional batteries in parallel for additional power backup.

4.14.2 Biometric and Keypad/PIN

Biometric access control systems are two-step validation systems used for high security access applications. They require the most time and the most information to process an individual.

- The individual seeking access first enters a unique PIN on a keypad. The PIN is used to find the person's biometric information on file. This information is then compared to the individual's actual biometric presentation (such as a hand print, fingerprint, voice print, or retina scan) given to the biometric reader at the access point. If the actual presentation is validated by the system, the individual is granted access.
- The most reliable biometric technologies are hand print, fingerprint, hand signature, and voice recognition. All of these require that users participate in a one-to-one initial enrollment session with the system administrator.

4.14.3 Card Access

There are four basic card technologies recommended: smart chip, proximity, magnetic stripe, and bar code.

In card access systems, it is the responsibility of employees and other card holders to immediately report any lost or stolen cards to security. If an unauthorized person uses a lost or stolen card to access a facility, that access event is recorded as access by the owner of the card. Access cards are no different than house keys or car keys—if the owner is careless and is burglarized as a result, the responsibility for the loss rests with the owner.

4.14.4 Card and Keypad/PIN

Many card access systems also offer numeric keypad features as additional options to their card readers.

- These systems are two-step validation systems that offer a higher level of access control and security. However, they require additional time for individuals to be processed.
- The typical access procedures for these systems require that the user present the card to the card reader and then enter a unique PIN on the numeric keypad.
- Many facilities elect to use only the card portion of the system during peak access hours. This helps the system maximize the number of individuals who can be processed during high-volume periods.
- During times of lower volumes, the use of a PIN as a second validation method provides protection against unreported lost or stolen cards.

4.14.5 Keypad/PIN Systems

There are quite a number of different keypad access systems available.

Keypad systems can either be electronic or mechanical. The keypad is used to enter an access code in mechanical systems and to enter the PIN in electronic systems. Electronic keypads are covered in the next section, but see the *Lock Systems* section for information on mechanical keypads.

For both systems, maintaining access integrity (the access code for a mechanical system and the individual PIN for an electronic system) is the single most important requirement.

For more information on the requirements of electronic access systems and the use of keypads and PINs, see the earlier section on *Alarm Systems*, especially the subtopics of *Panels* and *Control Units*.

4.14.5.1 Electronic Keypads

An electronic keypad requires a numeric code to activate the locking hardware to which it is attached. Be certain to select keypads that are designed for frequent use, are damage-resistant, and require infrequent maintenance. We recommend using a unique code or PIN for each authorized individual.

The best method for assigning PINs is to allow users to define their own. This helps people remember their access code. If a system operator assigns PINs, people tend to write the number down, which leads to a loss of integrity and generally less satisfied users.

Failure to delete old numbers from the system, or to update changed numbers, causes the most vulnerability in PIN systems.

To ensure an adequate level of security, we recommend that individuals change their PINs on a regular basis. This requires that the system has database options for adding, changing, and deleting numbers.

Follow the update procedures recommended for all PIN systems (see *Keypad/PIN Systems* immediately preceding this topic).

4.15 ESCORT POLICY

All nonemployees other than contract or service vendors are categorized as short-term visitors. Their identity and authorization to visit your organization must be verified. See the *Visitor Verification and Authorization* section later in this chapter.

- All short-term visitors must be escorted at all times while on your organization's premises.
- Escorts must be resident organization employees that represent the business area being visited.

4.16 FALSE ALARMS

Until recently, the security industry defined a false alarm as an alarm signal transmitted when no alarm condition exists. False alarms were classified according to the conditions that caused them:

- Environmental: rain, fog, wind, hail, lightning, heat, cold, and so forth
- Animals: rodents, insects, pets, large animals, etc.
- Man-made disturbances: sonic booms, vehicles, electromagnetic interference (EMI), etc.

- Equipment malfunction: component failures, transmission errors, line noise, etc.
- Operator errors
- Unknown causes

However, the idea of a false alarm poses several problems for today's security industry for the following reasons:

- All alarms must be processed as legitimate alarm conditions.
- All alarms have meaning because they are caused by events that must be accounted for, controlled, or removed. When a device malfunctions, an operator makes an error, or an unaccounted event such as an environmental occurrence causes an alarm condition, it indicates that some part of the system is not functioning as planned.
- The design of the system failed to take all conditions into consideration:
  - Training, management, and procedures need to be reviewed.
  - Components are failing in unexpected ways and they need to be adjusted, modified, or replaced with more reliable parts or systems.
- All facilities must focus on implementing security systems that are 100 percent reliable in terms of detecting real alarm conditions and not transmitting alarm signals when no alarm conditions exist.

4.17 FENCING

Fencing defines the company's spaces, both internal and external. It controls access to the company's property, directs internal traffic flow, and separates functions within the site or facility (e.g., the shipping and receiving function from will call). Fencing also discourages and delays intrusion.

Different business settings require different fencing applications:

- Industrial and manufacturing: use chain link or wire fabric fences.
- Offices: decorative fences are often requested. The height of the fence depends on the projected risk.
- Parking areas: use a system of low height steel posts or precast bollards for defining the perimeter; use electronic gates and controls at all entrances and exits to control vehicle access.

- Construction zone: use temporary wire fabric fencing to separate construction areas from existing organization property and facilities. The fence should be 6–8 feet high, have its own full-height gate, and be clearly marked with warning and notifications signs. Limit the number of gate openings to the amount required for construction operations.
- Hazardous areas: some areas are especially prone to vandalism, sabotage, or contain high safety risks for unauthorized personnel. Examples of these kinds of areas are: cooling towers, electrical substations, storage areas, processing controls and equipment, chemical tank farms, emergency power and communications, warehouses, and natural hazards. These areas, whether internal or external, require fencing, which may need to be integrated with alarm sensors, CCTV, security wire, patrols, and remote station monitoring.

4.17.1 Fencing Considerations

Fencing applications must meet the functional, environmental, and aesthetic requirements of their business settings.

- Height: Height depends on the projected risk to the area. To deter physical access (specifically, someone climbing over), use a seven-foot fence with V-rails or top rails. To create a general-control barrier, use a three- to six-foot fence with notifications and warnings.
- Drainage: Use culverts, tunnels, or manholes that extend under the fence. Secure all openings that are larger than 96 square inches.
- Clear zones: These must be at least three feet on both sides of the fence.
- Inspection and maintenance: Inspect the perimeter on a regular basis for gaps, holes, and cuts in the fence; accumulation of materials such as drum and pallets in the established clear zone; and growth of vegetation either inside the clear zone or projecting over the fence.

4.18 FIRE FILES

Fire files are designed to serve one purpose: fire protection. Papers not stored in fire files might be exposed to temperatures well in excess of 1,000 degrees Fahrenheit during a fire. Since paper chars at approximately 350 degrees Fahrenheit, there is a good possibility that paper records stored in a regular file cabinet will be destroyed during a fire. Fire files come in a variety of UL ratings.[1] A fire file with a one-hour fire rating is suitable for most applications.

4.19 GATES

Gates provide access control of vehicular and pedestrian traffic, both as they enter and exit a facility. Gates are breaks in a facility's perimeter barrier. They must provide the same level of protection as the rest of the barrier.

- Use as few gates as possible. Balance traffic flow needs with security requirements.
- Gates must be secured when not in use. Never leave an open gate unattended.
- Gates can be secured either electronically or with heavy-duty padlocks and case-hardened chains. Padlocks are now available with smart key options for audit trail. Where common-issue keys are used, minimize the number of keys and follow your organization's key control procedures.
- In gate areas, use your organization's engineering standards for lighting to ensure vehicle identification and access control.
- Inspect active and inactive gates on a regular basis for signs of tampering or breakdown. Repair problems promptly.
- Fire access gates must be locked and the local fire department must be given one copy of the key.

4.20 HUMAN INTERVENTION

In the past, organizations used human intervention whenever possible to control access. However, improvements in electronics and technology now make it feasible and cost effective to use electronic access control systems in lieu of human intervention. This applies only when entry configurations are designed to prevent access by piggybacking and tailgating, and when systems are integrated with video cameras and recorders to provide an audit trail.

[1]UL refers to the rating system of Underwriters Laboratories, a safety testing and certification organization. Visit www.ul.com for more information.

Such an electronic access control systems configuration effectively eliminates the need for human intervention without compromising security.

4.20.1 ID Badge System

There are two general types of badges: permanent photo IDs enclosed in laminated plastic, and temporary access credentials made of disposable paper.

Permanent badges are intended for full-time employees, short-term employees (students, temporary employees, technical aids, etc.), long-term visitors (trades, services, and temporary workers), and contract workers.

Temporary badges are intended for visiting employees who don't have an organization ID badge, and for use by long-term employees who have lost, misplaced, or forgotten their badge. Short-term visitors also use temporary badges. Some short-term visitors require an escort; some do not.

Temporary badges have three special features:

1. They are color coded so that they are easy to recognize from a distance. The color coding and labeling clearly displays whether the person wearing the badge requires an escort.
2. They are time sensitive and have a visible expiration date.
3. The name of the visitor is displayed.

The following rules and procedures are central to the effectiveness of your organization's ID or badge system:

- If a badge is lost or stolen, it must be reported immediately to security.
- Badges must be surrendered to your organization when an employee is terminated, or upon request of your organization.
- Badges are not transferable.
- Each person is authorized to have only one badge.

4.21 INTRUSION DETECTION SYSTEM

Intrusion detection is a broad topic; it represents and incorporates many physical security elements and options. Your intrusion detection system probably has some or all of the following:

- Alarm systems
  - Alarm monitoring

- · Alarm annunciation
- · Motion detection
- · Magnetic contact switches
- CCTV, with motion detection and recorders
- Designated employees
- Electronic access systems
- Employee awareness programs
- Escort policy and procedures
- ID or badge system
- Lock systems
- Patrols and rounds
- Receptionists
- Seals
- Security officers
- Security patrol systems

For more information on each of these elements and options, go to the detailed discussions presented elsewhere in this chapter.

4.22 LANDSCAPING

Attractive barriers can be created using landscaping elements such as trees, hedges, terracing, retaining walls, large planters, trenches, and channels. Landscaping can increase security while softening the hard-edge image projected by traditional barriers such as walls and fences.

Follow these basic rules when landscaping a site:

- Locate plants at least four feet from buildings to prevent people or objects from being concealed next to a building.
- Be certain that landscaping elements do not allow people to be concealed near walkways, recreational spaces, or parking areas.
- Be certain that trees and shrubs cannot be used to scale a fence or wall. See *Fencing* earlier in this chapter for more information.

Consult with your organization's security coordinator and engineering team when you consider landscaping.

4.23 LIGHTING

Proper lighting provides the visibility required for surveillance.

Use the following guidelines to design and maintain your lighting system.

- Interior lighting must be relatively subdued so that observation and surveillance of the exterior can be performed from the interior.
- Exterior lighting design must be integrated with landscaping features to ensure dark areas are not created.
- Ensure that nighttime parking areas, as well as paths, stairwells, and walkways, are well lit. Follow national lighting standards for parking areas.
- Consider using a control system that provides lighting flexibility to help you better manage energy consumption.
- Emergency lighting systems must include a back-up power source and secure switch boxes.
- Assign responsibility for turning lights on and off, unless the lights are controlled by a photo-sensitive or timing device.
- Areas, buildings, and functions that are critical to your operations (for example, power stations, transformers, pump houses, and tank farms) must be well illuminated.
- Be certain that external lights that are mounted low to the ground are tamper-resistant and protected against vandalism.
- In areas where there are cameras, or where there is a history of vandalism or intrusion, consider increasing lighting levels.
- Be certain that you meet all local codes that exceed national lighting standards.

4.23.1 Summary of Lighting Standard

The four main points which should be covered by your engineering department's lighting standard are summarized below.

- Open parking facilities, sidewalks, and other pedestrian areas should be lit to a minimum maintained level of 1 foot candle at ground level, with a uniformity ratio of 4:1 average to minimum.
- Covered parking facilities should have an average foot candle level of 5 at ground level, with a uniformity ratio of 4:1. Walls, ceilings, and other covered surfaces should be painted white or a light color for high reflectance values.
- Exterior lighting for primary entrances, emergency exits, and approaching walkways that are in service during nighttime and non-business hours should have an average foot candle level of 5 at ground level, with a uniformity ratio of 4:1.

- Stairways in parking ramps should have an average foot candle level of 10. Whenever possible, walls and other covered surfaces should be white or light colored.

4.24 LOCK SYSTEMS

Locks are the most essential component of many physical security applications; everything from doors to fence gates to cabinets and furniture use locks to provide physical security.

The following sections discuss the important aspects of lock systems:

- Combination locks
- Key control
- Lock and key
- Locking hardware and furniture
- Mechanical keypads

4.24.1 Combination Locks

Access to the combinations for combination locks must be tightly controlled.

- Combination locks are one of the least secure methods for controlling access. The main weakness with combination locks is the failure to follow the procedure for purging and updating combinations.
- Lock combinations should be changed periodically to minimize the risk of compromise and unauthorized access. We recommend changing the combinations at least once every 90 days.

See *Mechanical Keypads* later in this section for more information.

4.24.2 Key Control

Key control is essential to the security performance of a lock and key system. Effective key control supports the day-to-day performance of the system, and prolongs the useful life of the system. Key control procedures must be adhered to strictly, or the system is quickly compromised:

- If an audit trail is desired, but the cost of electronic access control is, for certain doors, cost prohibitive,[2] consider the option of a smart key/cylinder application. The cost of a removable core/smart

---

[2]The average cost of an electronic access controlled door is $2,500–$3,000 per door.

cylinder is less than $500 per cylinder and smart key assigned to individuals. By insertion of a control key, the event memory of the cylinder is downloaded into the control key for uploading into security's database for audit trail. The downside to the smart key option is that you will not have a door position alarm, should the door be held or propped open.

- Select a key system that prevents unauthorized duplication of keys.
- Assign a key coordinator to manage all key control requirements.
- Keys are your organization's property; they are assigned to individuals based on a business need.
- Develop an authorization process with management for assignment and issue of keys to individuals.
- Maintain accountability for each key that is assigned.
- Conduct periodic key validation reviews with individual key holders to account for all the keys that have been assigned, returned, and reassigned.
- Maintain a property return procedure that is coordinated with management to ensure that keys are returned from all individuals who are leaving the company, changing job assignments, or relocating within the company.
- Rekey any lock where all assigned keys cannot be accounted for. Consider the deployment of removable core key ways. With removable cores, security may change out a single cylinder or a series of cylinders with the use of a core control key. This approach eliminates the delay and lost time in making changes to your keyed locks due to security incidents that require immediate need to change a lock and keys. Ongoing maintenance and upgrades to your keying system are facilitated by the deployment of a removable core system.
- **Do not issue master keys**. Master keys should never leave the facility. They should be signed in and out on a daily basis. The loss of a master key is a costly mistake; the probability of such an occurrence must be minimized as much as possible.

4.24.3 Lock and Key

Lock and key systems are one of the most frequently used physical security applications. For many security needs, it is the most appropriate and cost effective solution. There are many lock and key systems available. Some examples include the following:

- Best Access (Stanley)
- MEDECO
- ASSA

Your organization's minimum lock and key standards should require the following features of the lock and key system:

- Heavy duty or commercial grade construction
- Tamper-resistant construction
- Key blanks registered to your organization and not available through any local hardware suppliers or key services

Lock and key systems have some limitations:

- Keys do not provide an audit trail of the time of access and of the identity of the person gaining access.
- The loss of keys, or the loaning of keys to unauthorized personnel, can severely compromise the system.
- Key blanks are not always easy to control. They must be available only from your organization.
- Unauthorized duplication of keys can compromise the system.

Lock and key applications require a fair amount of human attention. They are only as secure as the key control practices of the people involved in the system. See the previous *Key Control* subsection for more information on the procedures required for effective key control.

4.24.4 Locking Hardware and Furniture

Locking hardware and locking furniture is recommended to secure proprietary information, personal items, and items of value.

- Locking furniture includes file cabinets, lockers, wardrobes, desks, storage bins, and compartments.
- Additional locking hardware can be used to supplement furniture and storage containers that require increased security. Typical examples include locking bars for file cabinets and lock pads or straps for computers and other high-value equipment.

- Keys for locking hardware and furniture must be stored in a secure manner.
- The loss of a key must be reported and the lock in question must be rekeyed immediately.

See the previous *Key Control* subsection for more information on the procedures required for effective key control.

4.24.5 Mechanical Keypads

A mechanical keypad requires a numeric code to activate the locking hardware to which it is attached. This kind of system provides the lowest level of security. These systems are **not recommended**.

A typical mechanical system uses a 3-, 4-, or 5-digit common code.

- You must change the code on a frequent basis in order for this kind of system to have any security value as a lock. Codes are easily exchanged between individuals, which compromises the system.
- A common or shared access code is not recommended, since no audit trail is provided with this approach. If you must use a common access code, change the number at least once every 90 days.

For more information, see the *Combination Locks* subsection earlier in this section.

4.25 MATERIAL PASSES

Material passes are recommended for controlling removal and return of your organization's equipment and material from your organization's facilities.

- Material passes require your organization's authorization.
- Your organization's authorizers are supervisors and/or managers responsible for the specific equipment or material to be removed.
- An audit trail must be kept that records the organization's business activities that justify the removal of your organization's property.

4.26 NATURAL BARRIERS

Natural barriers, such as rivers, lakes, cliffs, rock formations, and difficult terrain, can be used to provide a part of a facility's perimeter if they meet the facility's physical security requirements.

- Natural barriers by themselves are rarely adequate for providing complete physical access control.
- Most successful perimeter systems integrate natural barriers with constructed systems such as landscaping, fencing, signage, lighting, CCTV, and perimeter alarms.

4.27 PATROLS AND ROUNDS

Patrols and rounds are typically conducted by security officers for the purposes of inspection, response, verification, and reporting of a facility's operating and safety conditions. The typical duties and responsibilities of security officers on patrols and rounds include:

- Responses to emergencies such as fire, medical, spills, hazardous conditions, and other emergencies
- Alarm monitoring and reporting
- Protection of your organization's personnel and property
- Escort services to personnel
- Random inspections of predetermined areas or operations
- General inspections and integrity testing of security systems and monitoring points
- Conducting patrols and checking specific assigned points, often with the aid of a point monitoring system

See *Security Patrol Systems* later in this chapter for more information on the technology components of the systems.

4.28 RECEPTIONISTS

Receptionists play an important role as goodwill ambassadors for your organization when they greet guests, visitors, vendors, and employees. Your organization's positive image is enhanced when receptionists provide information and assistance in a courteous and timely manner. They also can perform important security functions, such as access control and verification of authorization.

- Receptionists require customer service and communications training.
- Provide receptionists with clear written guidelines and procedures.
- Be certain that the receptionist has the sign-in logs and authorization lists required by the position.

- The reception area must have a direct line of sight to the outside.
- Elevate the security or reception station at least six inches to facilitate vision and communications control.
- To help direct and control people traffic, provide physical guides and barriers such as rope stanchions, plantings, low panels, or partitions.

4.29 RESTRICTED AREAS

Restricted areas are all internal organization spaces and external spaces that require special access control such that access is granted to only those individuals who work within the space or who are authorized to visit.

- These areas are typically controlled by card access, which provides the most reliable security.
- It is important to limit the number of entry and exit points. The fewer, the better.
- Use proper signage to notify people of the boundaries of a restricted area.
- Use CCTV cameras with time-lapse video recorders, integrated with the card access system, whenever possible. We recommend this approach whenever entry of unauthorized personnel or difficulty with verification of individuals is an issue for the area.

4.30 ROOF ACCESS

The roof must be accessible only from the interior of the building. Where exterior ladders are provided, they must be retracted to a height of more than 10 feet above the ground and locked when not in use.

- Laboratory facilities with chemical exhaust systems often require access control for the roof area.
- Either lock and key and electronic access control systems can be used to control roof access.
- Using local annunciation of alarms and access logs as part of your system for controlling roof access is recommended.

4.31 SAFES

Safe containers are used to protect and secure restricted information, sensitive information, and high-value materials from unauthorized access and damage.

- Safes are tested and rated separately for both burglary and fire protection.
- To determine the level of protection required for your business or government application, refer to the appropriate industry or government guidelines.
- Safes that are designed for the residential market are inadequate because they offer a level of protection approximately equal to a locked file cabinet or desk.

4.32 SEALS

Seals are used to monitor the continuous required locking of a barrier, container, or door. Broken seals indicate that the barrier, container, or door was opened without the consent of the people responsible for controlling access.

- Your supply of seals and related materials must be safeguarded against unauthorized use.
- Seals provide minimal security. They are recommended only as a basic, low-cost security measure, or for temporary or emergency monitoring. See *Alarm Systems* earlier in this chapter for more information.

There are two common types of seals:

1. Lead seals, which are attached to a wire, imprinted with a code, and pressed in place with a pliers-like tool.
2. Paper seals, which are labels printed with unique patterns and codes and are attached with a nonrelease adhesive.

Seals have several limitations:

- A broken seal does not tell you when or how often a violation occurred during the period between the times it was checked.
- Seals require periodic checks, which means there must be security patrols to monitor the system.
- The frequency with which the seals are checked must be increased whenever a broken seal is discovered.

4.33 SECURITY DESKS

A security desk is a work station for security officers. The officers perform key security functions and they play an important role as goodwill ambassadors for your organization when they greet guests, visitors, vendors, and employees. Your organization's positive image is enhanced when they provide information and assistance in a courteous and timely manner.

A typical guard desk configuration includes space for telephones, log books and sign-in sheets, file storage, badging materials, door controls, radio equipment, CCTV monitors, recorders, and controls, intercom, alarm and access control terminals and printers, emergency and medical supplies, and a place to meet the public.

- The security desk area must have a direct line of sight to the outside.
- Position the desk for optimum control over human access and customer interaction.
- Elevate the desk area for increased visibility and communications control.
- Design the desk area for handicap access.
- To help direct and control people traffic, provide physical guides and barriers such as rope stanchions, plantings, low panels, or partitions.
- Provide sign-in logs and authorization lists.
- Provide clear written guidelines and procedures for the security officers.
- Be certain that the security officers receive customer service and communications training.

4.34 SECURITY OFFICERS

Security officers have duties and responsibilities that vary widely from site to site. However, it is important to remember that the primary duties of your security officers are access control, emergency response, alarm monitoring, systems maintenance, communications, and employee assistance.

Security officers, like receptionists, play an important role as goodwill ambassadors for your organization when they greet guests, visitors, vendors, and employees. Your organization's positive image is enhanced when they provide information and assistance in a courteous and timely manner.

The keys to an effective security force are as follows:

- Clear security policies and procedures. These provide a foundation that tells security personnel (e.g., security officers, receptionists, designated employees, etc.) what they must do to properly operate and manage the security technologies involved in their security system as well as what they must do to avoid the liabilities of nonperforming systems or negative security due to inappropriate responses.
- Regular training, both on-the-job training and systems training.
- Frequent systems validation and testing.
- Professionalism: the human element, and its integration into the security system, determines the system's overall effectiveness.

4.35 SECURITY PATROL SYSTEMS

Security patrol systems are electronic and mechanical devices designed to monitor specific points or areas of a facility that require the presence of a security officer.

- The officer uses the device to make contact, at specific designated times, with physical location points at various security positions in the facility.
- The security control system records the time of the contact, and the status of the point. Observations regarding security or safety issues can also be recorded.
- Patrol reports are required for security management and safety. Insurance carriers often require these reports as well.
- Security patrol systems can effectively integrate surveillance by officers with mechanical and electronic verification devices, such as time clocks and bar code readers. To be most effective, such patrol systems must allow for change and flexibility.
  - Hard-wired stations points that are built into the structure and/or require the officer to be present at a specific time are not recommended. Mechanical devices, such as bar code readers, are both less expensive and more easily moved to other sites than are hard-wired points.
  - Hand-held security patrol wands that engage the station points, record the action, and provide downloadable data provide both documented observations and archival records for analysis and reporting.

See the *Patrols and Rounds* section earlier in this chapter for more information.

4.36 SIGNS

Signs are used as the first level of control in physical security systems.

- Signs provide information and are a key element in communication between your organization and the people who work at and visit the company.
- Signs also provide instructions and are used to mitigate liabilities. They define areas of operation and control access to restricted areas.

Be certain that your signs are worded carefully to avoid statements that imply security protection or performance beyond that which is provided. For example, statements such as "This area *protected* by (or *secured* by) closed circuit television" may imply performance that is not delivered.

- Check with your organization's legal counsel before you post a new sign.
- Ask your management and facility security committee to review the signs in your business for the appropriate applications of signs in support of your operational and security needs.
- Postings that relate to inspection guidelines need to be carefully reviewed.

4.37 VISITOR VERIFICATION AND AUTHORIZATION

Before any individual who is not part of your organization's authorized personnel can gain access to a facility, their identity must be verified and authorization for access provided by designated, authorized organization personnel. See the *Authorizer Lists* and *Escort Policy* sections earlier in this chapter for more information.

4.38 WALLS

Walls are the most fundamental element of physical security. Walls are used as barriers, to define property lines, and as a basic architectural component for support and shelter.

- Walls must be designed and constructed to specifications defined by the security requirements of the assets they protect.

- Most walls use hardened materials, are built to a specific thickness and height, and have a small number of openings. A typical design for a secure office uses walls that are full height (i.e., they reach from the floor to floor above) to prevent anyone from crawling over the top or down through a suspended ceiling.
- Precious materials and cash require reinforced walls made of steel and concrete.
- Laboratories are normally built with concrete or glazed block at full height to contain fires, contaminated emissions, and environmental hazards.
- In plants, walls are used to visually and acoustically isolate restricted areas of production from unauthorized areas. In addition, these walls are used to restrict physical access, provide fire and emissions protection, and isolate special environments such as clean rooms.
- Computer rooms need walls that provide both security and environmental protection.

Facilities that have new construction or remodeling planned must carefully consider how the new and existing walls fit into the overall design and use of the total facility. Operational and physical security requirements of adjoining spaces may not be well served by the new spaces and its level of construction.

Prior to construction, have the facilities security committee review the construction plans for security issues relating to the new space and to the effects of the new space on the adjoining spaces and their operations (for example, traffic flow, doors, windows, ductwork, ceilings).

4.39 WINDOWS

For security and operational purposes, limit the number and size of windows in a building. Windows at the perimeter of the property and/or at ground level must be protected with some or all of the following:

- Security laminated film or lexan/polycarbonate glazing
- Decorative metal grills
- Laminated heavy gauge wire mesh
- Alarm monitoring, glass break detection devices, and annunciation. See the *Alarm Systems* section earlier in this chapter for further information.
- All windows that open to a nonsecure area must be secured from the inside with locking hardware.

CHAPTER 5

Systems Implementation and Evaluation

5.1 INTRODUCTION

This chapter contains guidelines for security system implementation and evaluation. The following topics are covered:

- Selecting a security system
- Selecting a vendor or supplier
- System installation
- Turn-on period
- System testing, evaluation, and validation
- Policies and procedures

5.2 SELECTING A SECURITY SYSTEM

This section discusses the three most important activities you should engage in prior to selecting a security system:

1. Collecting the right kind of information
2. Considering purchasing options relevant to your needs
3. Preparing system plans and specifications

5.2.1 Collecting Information

Product information must be collected on all aspects of the security system prior to purchase. Although the vendors will supply you with a great deal of product information, you should not rely solely on their advice when making product selections. Start collecting information early in the planning and design process.

There are many sources available that can provide you with advice and assistance as you evaluate product information, including:

- Your organization's engineering department;
- Your organization's purchasing department;
- Other similar facilities of your company;
- Peer companies; and
- Professional organizations.

5.2.2 Purchasing Considerations

Before you purchase a system, use your available resources to address the following considerations:

How financially stable is the vendor? Many companies in the security business do not have long-term stability; every year there are some that go out of business. Verify the references provided by the vendor.

How well does the proposed system interface with other current and planned systems? Does the proposed system fit with your organization's culture and business operations?

Do the options and features you're considering meet your long-term objectives? Be careful not to purchase features you don't need. In addition, look for flexibility and modularity in the system so that future needs can be accommodated through system expansion rather than system replacement.

What sort of performance history does the product have? Has it been shown to be reliable and of high quality?

What warranties and guaranties are offered with the product?

Be certain to look at the service and maintenance issues: Is local support available? What is the service record of the vendor? Are cost-effective service contracts available?

What is the value to price ratio for the product? Is it a cost effective solution for your situation? What are the purchase vs. lease trade-offs in price?

Is the product available in a timely manner? Will delivery and installation meet your schedule?

5.2.3 Preparing System Plans and Specifications

Before you begin the vendor selection process, put together a document that describes the user requirements and functional design of the security system. This document should:

- Outline what the system will accomplish from the user's point of view;
- Describe how the system will fit into the business and how it will enhance the operations;

- List, in general terms, what the system components will be; and
- Describe the customer's (your) performance expectations for the system.

This document is the first step in designing a security system. It is the primary tool for interviewing vendors, as it helps you direct vendor efforts toward your goals, rather than relying on vendors to provide direction.

As you begin to work with potential vendors, you will be able to refine the system plans and specifications. Eventually, you will have a document that provides specific design instructions to the vendor(s) you choose to work with.

5.3 SELECTING A VENDOR OR SUPPLIER

As you select a vendor or supplier, be certain that the vendor can meet the local needs of your business. Look for vendors with experience in multiple areas, and choose a primary vendor who will be responsible for the final operation of the system.

5.3.1 Meeting Local Needs

A vendor must be able to meet local needs and support local conditions of your business.

- Buying from a big name in the industry does not always ensure that they have an office close to your business. If your organization's locations are in small towns, make sure to find out whether the vendor has quick access to these areas.
- Check with other companies in your location to find out if a particular vendor is doing a good job of meeting their local needs.

5.3.2 Evaluating Potential Vendors

Look for vendors that have experience with multiple systems and with systems integration. For example, look for a vendor with experience in access control, CCTV, alarm points, door hardware, and intercom controls.

5.3.3 Choose a Primary Vendor

We recommend using a primary vendor for all your security systems whenever possible. Good primary vendors are those that handle a wide line of leading and well-established security products, and provide multiple services, including systems integration.

- The primary vendor is responsible for the final operations of the system. That vendor has ultimate responsibility for integrating the purchased system with components of the existing system, the system's overall performance, resolving problems and issues, and future service and warranty concerns.
- Avoid purchasing system components that lead to fragmentation or isolation of parts of the system. Plan for a multi-faceted operation.
- Before choosing a primary vendor, be certain to assess the long-term stability of the vendor's organization.

5.3.4 Relationships with Primary Vendors

Primary vendors often take on one of three main roles: system installation, systems integration, and systems team leader. The primary vendor is responsible for providing your organization with as-built drawings when the system is complete.

- For small systems, the primary vendor often supplies all the components and performs the installation. In other cases, the vendor will supply the drawings to an outside contractor who won the bid, or to the plant's resident engineering department, who then completes the installation.
- For larger systems, the primary vendor acts as a systems integrator, hires all other vendors and contractors, and coordinates the various parts of the job for your organization. The primary vendor in cases like this is often a company that specializes in security systems installations.
- For full-scale systems, the primary vendor acts as the team leader and liaison to your organization's engineering department and the facility's resident engineer. Drawings are supplied by the primary vendor or your organization prior to installation.

5.4 SYSTEM INSTALLATION

System installation requires a plan to address design issues. In addition, all subcontractor companies and their personnel must meet your organization's requirements, the system must be bench tested, and the primary vendor is required to supply as-built drawings for the system.

5.4.1 Design Issues

Three key features of successful system operation are often overlooked during the installation design:

1. Testing the system
2. Training the operators, including initial and follow-up training, and cross-training for backup
3. Training the users

5.4.2 Subcontractor and Installer Requirements

All subcontractors and installers must be screened and approved by your organization.

- An installer must have a minimum of five years of installation experience and a number of positive references from reputable peer companies with similar projects.
- Subcontractor requirements apply both to the installation company and its individual personnel.
- All vendors, suppliers, and subcontractors must comply with your organization's performance guidelines for site access and security.

5.4.3 Bench Testing

All system components that will be installed at your site must first be bench tested:

- They must be loaded and operational at the vendor's location
- They must be inspected and approved by your organization at that location
- They must be tested at your facility after they have been installed

5.4.4 As-Built Drawings

One of the areas frequently neglected in the purchase and installation of security systems is a set of **as-built drawings** (i.e., good documentation from the vendors on the systems as they have actually been installed). As-built drawings include the following:

- Layout drawings
- System block diagrams and riser diagrams
- Wiring typicals

- Elementaries
- Panel schedules
- Panel wiring diagrams

The most important aspects of the as-built drawings package are the diagrams that show accurate field locations of the devices and any field modifications to the generic wiring and layouts.

The set of as-built drawings is a critical part of the total documentation package required from the primary vendor, which also includes:

- Performance specifications for the system and how it meets or exceeds customer requirements;
- Cut-sheets on each device and major system component;
- Standard system configuration drawings and sketches;
- Required or recommended wiring types;
- System operations documentation; and
- Training materials

5.5 TURN-ON PERIOD

The turn-on period must be planned and implemented in conjunction with the development of policies and procedures that support the system.

5.5.1 Planning Considerations

Allow sufficient time in your implementation plan to accommodate the schedules required for:

- Facilities construction;
- Initial testing;
- Occupancy; and
- Training.

5.5.2 Initial Testing

Your system must be operational prior to having personnel and business processes use the system.

- Initial testing must occur before the new premises or remodeled areas are occupied.

- Risks associated with testing are minimized by performing initial testing prior to occupancy.
- Training is enhanced when initial testing is conducted in accordance with the overall implementation plan. A completely functional system provides the best training environment.

5.5.3 Training

Training consists of both an initial training phase and a follow-up phase.

- Initial training is usually a minimum of eight hours, with the training requirements determined by management.
- Follow-up training occurs approximately 90 days after initial training, with the minimum requirements for the training determined by local organization management.
- The integration of the new system, its components, and equipment with the facility's operational procedures is a critical aspect of training, both initial and follow-up. A walk-through, with hands-on equipment presentation, is a fundamental part of integration training.
- Cross-training the primary operators and the secondary operators is important for covering personnel issues such as vacation and sick days.
- Depending on your operations, user training may also be required.

Training documentation includes:

- Manufacturer's owner manuals or system operations manuals;
- Copies of the training presentation materials used by the systems integrator or prime vendor; and
- Training materials, such as written procedures, checklists, and training handouts.

5.6 SYSTEM TESTING, EVALUATION, AND VALIDATION

System evaluation includes measuring the final system against its initial performance goals as well as performing ongoing testing to see that the system continues to meet those goals.

5.6.1 System Objectives

System evaluation is required to assess whether the system is meeting the objectives it was designed to meet, such as:

- Controlling access;
- Identifying people in specific areas;
- Detecting unauthorized entry; and
- Detecting motion in restricted areas.

5.6.2 Testing, Measurements and System's Commissioning

Standard testing and measurement procedures for evaluating a system include the following:

- Every device and system's configuration, including the software and setup, definitions, rules and coschedules, must be tested for timing, performance, and high reliability with an attempt to force the device and its integrated peripherals to fail. Failures must be evaluated as to the cause, and the errors must be corrected. Relying on the primary vendor is a consideration, but a separate contract with an outside systems specialist is an effective solution to holding the primary vendor accountable for its work, attention to detail, and applied best practices in its installation. The generation of an independent punch list is strongly recommended. Ten percent should be withheld in the primary vendor's contract until all punch list items have been rectified.
- Measuring the response levels at the lowest set point of an alarm: When the alarm is triggered, measure the response provided by the alarm company or the system operators,
- Testing contact points by opening doors.
- Testing the system under different conditions and during different times or shifts.

5.6.3 Validation

Use the following additional validation techniques.

- Check the recordings provided by cameras in access control areas to determine that people can be visually identified.
- Test the sensitivity of motion detectors by having security personnel try to avoid being noticed in the areas protected by these detectors.
- Use invalid access cards on doors. Try old cards on doors for which they are no longer supposed to work.

- Open doors to verify that alarm sensors initiate alarms and that alarm annunciation occurs.

5.6.4 Maintenance and Record Keeping
Ongoing validation includes ongoing testing and record keeping.

- Establish a testing schedule.
- Keep permanent records of the results of the tests.
- Perform periodic checks to determine whether the schedule is being followed.

5.7 POLICIES AND PROCEDURES

All systems must be supported by policies and procedures. Security systems are most affected by your organization's policies and ethical standards.

5.7.1 Your Organization's Policies
Many of the policies and procedures enacted by your organization will likely impact security.

- Security systems are meant to enhance and transparently complement your organization's human resource principles, employee codes of conduct, business conduct policy, and local operating procedures.
- Additionally, security is meant to enhance safety, benefit environmental concerns and industrial hygiene, and provide guidelines for shipping, receiving, and distribution channels.

5.7.2 Ethical and Regulatory Standards
Security systems must always conform with regulatory requirements and be operated in an ethical and legal manner.

- Guidelines provided by agencies such as the Occupational Safety and Health Administration (OSHA) and National Fire Protection Association (NFPA), and regulatory standards such as UL and the Americans with Disabilities Act (ADA), to mention a few, must be designed into the performance guidelines of your organization's security systems.
- Legal concerns can be addressed with the assistance of your company's legal counsel and security coordinator.

CHAPTER 6

Physical Security Resources

6.1 INTRODUCTION

This chapter contains information about resources available to assist you as you address physical security issues. These include:

- Internal resources;
- External resources;
- Educational resources;
- Publications;
- Professional organizations;
- And professional certification.

6.2 INTERNAL RESOURCES

The three main types of internal resources that will be available to you for concerns of physical security are

- Your organization's departments;
- Your organization's publications; and
- Your organization's facilities security program.

6.2.1 Your Organization's Departments

There are many departments that can regularly provide support and assistance in security-related matters

- Engineering (for lighting services and security project work)
- Information Technology (for computer systems and integration, software and hardware, and for security procedures)
- Safety
- Risk Management
- Telecommunications

6.2.2 Your Organization's Publications

It's likely that your organization already publishes internal documents that may contain information on security guidelines and related information. These publications may include:

- Publications on your company's information security procedures; and
- Personnel security guidelines.

6.2.3 The Facility Security Program

Annual US business losses related to crime regularly number in the tens of billions. Most organizations, unfortunately, have not escaped this growing problem. Although the number of crime-related incidents has not increased dramatically, the cost per incident continues to rise. However, the losses to the company can be contained and controlled through greater efforts at proactive security measures.

One such proactive security measure is to develop a facility security risk assessment program to assist your company's management reduce both the internal and external losses to the company. This kind of program provides an organized approach at all organization facilities. It takes into consideration both the basic security objectives of the security team as well as the needs and business goals of your organization's management.

Key aspects of a facility security risk management program include:

- The appointment of a facility security coordinator;
- A site-specific security committee;
- A survey of vulnerability issues;
- The inclusion of security issues in yearly sector reviews;
- Evaluations of security systems effectiveness;
- Integration of security systems and programs with operations;
- Policy and procedures reviews and modifications as required;
- Facility security modifications as required by changing business environments; and
- Training and education for personnel with security responsibilities.

6.3 EXTERNAL RESOURCES

In addition to the internal resources available to you, there are several external resources from which you can benefit:

- Peer companies
- Local security professionals

6.3.1 Peer Companies

Peer companies are your company-approved organizations with locations near you. These organizations have similar operations and security concerns, and may prove useful as a source of information and advice. Some of the items you may want to review with a peer company include:

- Business operations and facility planning;
- Security systems and practices;
- History of incidents;
- Security personnel, functions, and job descriptions;
- Hardware and software systems; and
- Vendors and suppliers.

6.3.2 Local Security Professionals

Local security professionals can:

- Share programs, information, and resources;
- Help you locate people with similar operations and problems;
- Provide experiences and resources that are currently part of your organization's knowledge base; and
- Provide information on issues and trends.

6.4 EDUCATIONAL RESOURCES

A number of educational opportunities exist, both nationally and internationally, for those people in your business who have been assigned security responsibilities.

There are several different options available to you:

- Individual programs
- Training programs
- Degree programs

6.4.1 Individual Programs

ASIS International offers a series of courses, seminars, and workshops. The following programs are particularly useful for security personnel:

- Assets Protection I and II. These two courses provide a broad overview of security theory and practices.

- The Certified Protection Professional (CPP) Review Course. This course provides a review for the CPP exam, and is an excellent review course for all security professionals.
- The ASIS Annual Seminar and Exhibits. This event combines educational programs on a broad spectrum of security topics, forums for security policy makers and experts, and displays of the latest technology and service offerings from security vendors.

6.4.2 Training Programs

Training is available from a number of professional security organizations.

- Physical security systems training includes topics such as the design and operation of security systems, CCTV, alarms, access control, keys, and badging ID systems.
- Functional training is also available in areas such as technology theft prevention, information security, uniformed officers supervision, emergency planning and response, and warehousing, transportation, and distribution security.
- The ASIS National Standing Committee on Physical Security also offers regularly scheduled training opportunities.

6.5 PUBLICATIONS

There are several major categories of publications that deal with physical security issues:

- ASIS International's Information Resources Center (IRC)[1]
- Periodicals and journals
- Books

The number of security-related periodicals, journals, books, and other publications has dramatically increased over the past ten years. It's now possible to find information on a specific topic or provide general assistance if you are looking to expand your base of information.

The rest of this section provides a list of recommended reading materials for people with security responsibilities.

[1]Visit https://www.asisonline.org/Membership/Library/Pages/default.aspx for more information about the IRC.

6.5.1 ASIS International's Information Resources Center

The ASIS International Information Resources Center (IRC) has publications with material common to all core security disciplines as well as material for specialty areas. The IRC has copies of materials to lend, and, in some cases, copies for on-site reference use only. Some of the material may be purchased through the ASIS website.

6.5.2 Periodicals and Journals

We recommend the following journals and newsletters:

- *Computer Security Digest*
- *Forensic Accounting Review*
- *The Security Industry Newsletter*
- *Corporate Security Letter*
- *Access Control*
- *Information Security*
- *Physical Control*

6.5.3 Books

We recommend several books as general background information for the field of physical security.

- *The Protection of Assets Manual*, ASIS International
  https://poa.asisonline.org/Pages/default.aspx.
- *Effective Physical Security*, 4th edition, by Lawrence Fennelly, Butterworth-Heinemann, 2012.
  http://store.elsevier.com/product.jsp?isbn=9780124158924.
- *Security and Loss Prevention*, 6th edition, by Philip Purpura, Butterworth-Heinemann, 2013.
  http://store.elsevier.com/product.jsp?isbn=9780123878465.
- *Crime Prevention Through Environmental Design*, 3rd edition, by Lawrence Fennelly and Timothy Crowe, Butterworth-Heinemann, 2013.
  http://store.elsevier.com/product.jsp?locale=en_US&isbn=9780124116351.

Other books offered through Elsevier's Security Executive Council Risk Management Portfolio that complement the *Physical Security Strategy and Process Playbook* include the *Reducing Personnel Security Risks Playbook* and *Workplace Security Playbook*. For more information about each of these titles, visit: http://store.elsevier.com/coArticle.jsp?pageid=15300002.

6.6 PROFESSIONAL ORGANIZATIONS

It's highly recommended that the person who has been assigned security responsibility at your facility join ASIS International. There are also other organizations available for specialized interests, which are described in the subsection below.

6.6.1 ASIS International

- ASIS International has more than 38,000 members worldwide. ASIS members are dedicated to protecting the people, property, and the information assets of a diverse group of public and private organizations. There is probably a local chapter in which you can participate.
- Local ASIS chapters are designed to provide local contacts for the people assigned primary security responsibilities for their organizations.
- ASIS members receive two publications each month, opportunities for training, and a wealth of security information.

6.6.2 Other Organizations for Specialized Interests

For other, more specialized interests, the following organizations are available:

- Association of Certified Fraud Examiners (ACFE)
  http://www.acfe.com/.
- International Association of Professional Security Consultants (IAPSC)
  http://iapsc.org/.
- Communications Fraud Control Association (CFCA)
  http://www.cfca.org/about.php.
- Door and Hardware Institute: Distributors of doors and builders' hardware; architectural consultants.
  http://www.dhi.org/.
- Institute of Internal Auditors
  http://www.theiia.org/.
- International Society of Crime Prevention Practitioners
  http://www.iscpp.org/.

6.7 PROFESSIONAL CERTIFICATION

ASIS International sponsors the Certified Protection Professional (CPP) program for the advancement of the security profession.

* Candidates for the CPP credential must meet educational and experience requirements and pass a written examination.
* Membership in ASIS is not a prerequisite.
* Certified professionals must qualify for recertification every three years through educational and other professional development activities.

6.7.1 Eligibility Prerequisites

Each person applying to the Certified Protection Professional (CPP) program must meet the following basic standards:

* Ten years of security experience, at least half of which shall have been in responsible charge of a security function; or
* An earned associate's degree from an accredited college and eight years of security experience, at least half of which shall have been in responsible charge of a security function; or
* An earned bachelor's degree from an accredited college or university and five years of security experience, at least half of which shall have been in responsible charge of a security function; or
* An earned master's degree from an accredited college or university and four years of security experience, at least half of which shall have been in responsible charge of a security function; or
* An earned doctoral degree from an accredited college or university and three years of security experience, at least half of which shall have been in responsible charge of a security function.

6.7.2 Examination

Written examinations are required for all applicants who meet the experience and education requirements. Successful achievement of passing grades on a battery of tests is necessary.

The exam covers 21 subject areas in total, though not all 21 need be known to every applicant. The applicant's test shall include the eight mandatory areas (i.e., the core knowledge subject areas) and four specialty areas chosen by the applicant from the optional subject areas.

6.7.3 Core Knowledge Subject Areas

The ASIS CPP program has the following eight core knowledge subject areas:

1. Emergency planning
2. Investigations
3. Legal aspects
4. Personal security
5. Physical security
6. Protection of sensitive information
7. Security management
8. Substance abuse

6.7.4 Specialty Subject Areas

There are thirteen available specialty subject areas for optional study:

1. Banking and financial institutions
2. Computer security
3. Credit card security
4. Department of Defense security requirements
5. Educational institution security
6. Fire resources management
7. Health care institution security
8. Manufacturing security
9. Nuclear security
10. Public utility security
11. Restaurant and lodging security
12. Retail security
13. Transportation and cargo security

ABOUT THE CONTRIBUTING EDITOR

John Kingsley-Hefty is an experienced security consultant whose leadership, accountability, communication skills, and project management experience in security, facility design, building types, operations, programs, and products has spearheaded team success stories for clients' critical corporate initiatives to advance growth and competitive advantage.

As a registered architect, John's strategic vision and planning reduces security costs by advancing security into the preliminary building design process. For over 35 years John has been successfully providing security and design services to diverse organizations such as 3M, Chicago Tribune Companies, and St. Jude Medical, Inc.

John's area of expertise is physical security architecture.

About Elsevier's Security Executive Council Risk Management Portfolio

Elsevier's Security Executive Council Risk Management Portfolio is the voice of the security leader. It equips executives, practitioners, and educators with research-based, proven information and practical solutions for successful security and risk management programs. This portfolio covers topics in the areas of risk mitigation and assessment, ideation and implementation, and professional development. It brings trusted operational research, risk management advice, tactics, and tools to business professionals. Previously available only to the Security Executive Council community, this content—covering corporate security, enterprise crisis management, global IT security, and more—provides real-world solutions and "how-to" applications. This portfolio enables business and security executives, security practitioners, and educators to implement new physical and digital risk management strategies and build successful security and risk management programs.

The Security Executive Council (www.securityexecutivecouncil.com) is a leading problem-solving research and services organization focused on helping businesses build value while improving their ability to effectively manage and mitigate risk. Drawing on the collective knowledge of a large community of successful security practitioners, experts, and strategic alliance partners, the Council develops strategy and insight and identifies proven practices that cannot be found anywhere else. Their research, services, and tools are focused on protecting people, brand, information, physical assets, and the bottom line.

Elsevier (www.elsevier.com) is an international multimedia publishing company that provides world-class information and innovative solutions tools. It is part of Reed Elsevier, a world-leading provider of professional information solutions in the science, medical, risk, legal, and business sectors.